Luscious Landscapes

Simple Techniques for Dynamic Quilts

Joyce R. Becker

C&T PUBLISHING

© 2003 Joyce Becker

Editor-in-Chief: Darra Williamson

Editor: Cyndy Lyle Rymer

Technical Editor: Gael Betts/Joyce Lytle

Copyeditor/Proofreader: Gael Betts/Stacy Chamness/Carol Barrett

Cover Designer: Christina D. Jarumay

Design Director/Book Designer: Kristy A. Konitzer

Illustrator: Jeffery Carrillo

Production Assistant: Tim Manibusan

Photography: Sharon Risedorph unless otherwise noted

Published by C&T Publishing, Inc., P.O. Box 1456, Lafayette, California 94549

Front cover: *Here Chickee, Chickee, Chickee* (page 56) by Joyce Becker, photo by Mark Frey

Back cover: *English Garden* (page 41) by Joyce Becker

Library of Congress Cataloging-in-Publication Data

Becker, Joyce R.
 Luscious landscapes : simple techniques for dynamic quilts / Joyce R. Becker.
  p. cm.
Includes index.
 ISBN 1-57120-194-7 (paper trade)
 1. Machine appliqué. 2. Machine quilting. 3. Quilts. 4. Fabric pictures. 5. Landscape in art. I. Title.
TT779 .B397 2003
746.46'041--dc21
                2002015143

Printed in China

10 9 8 7 6 5 4

Acknowledgments

To my husband, Donald, my trusted friend and soul mate. Thank you for being my cheerleader, my unpaid assistant, for lugging my bags, my quilts, my projector, and all of my supplies to places far and wide. Most of all, thank you for your valuable critique when needed.

Our sons, Shawn and Shane, I love you more than words can say. I am very proud of you and thank you for supporting my art. To my stepchildren: Bev, Mark, Don, Mike, and Kim. Thank you for accepting and welcoming me into your lives and supporting my quilting ventures. To my grandchildren: Matteline, Wendy, Shelbie, Logan, and Jenny. You brighten my day and bring me so much joy.

To my parents, Ima Jo and Bill Burgreen, thank you for instilling the belief that each of your children could become anything they desired, as long as they tried. To my twin sister, Jan White, and to all of my siblings; Bobby, Jerry, and Charlotte, thank you for your valuable input. Life has taken each of us on a different path.

To my long-term circle of "Thursday Group" quilting friends, especially Patti, Rosy, and Denise. You're always there for me. How can I find the words to tell you how very much your continued support, help, and friendship means to me except to say "Thank you?"

To Melanie Duyungan, your friendship and "big picture" suggestions regarding my book proposal are highly appreciated. To Jane Moxey, you brighten my life and I thank you for your suggestions regarding my book design and layout.

To the guest artists and students who so generously allowed me to showcase their works of art in this book. Thank you for sharing your quilts, your techniques, and your words of wisdom. To my dear friend, Sonia Grasvik, I am forever in your debt for letting me include your incredible fine finishing techniques in this book.

Thanks to the vendors who provided me with materials and products: Sulky of America, SkyDyes, 505 Spray and Fix, Material Resources Fabric Collection, Artfabrik, and Hoffman Fabrics. Thanks to the incredible staff at C&T; Todd Hensley, Cyndy Rymer, Diane Pedersen, Gael Betts, Mari Dreyer, Tim Manibusan, Kristy Konitzer, and Jeffery Carrillo.

CONTENTS

INTRODUCTION 4

Chapter One THE BASICS 6

Chapter Two SELECT A DESIGN INSPIRATION 11

Chapter Three READY, SET, GO 18

Chapter Four BASTE AND EMBELLISH 26

Chapter Five ADD TEXTURE WITH MACHINE EMBROIDERY 36

PROJECTS

Chapter Six LUSCIOUS LITTLE LANDSCAPES 40

Chapter Seven SENSATIONAL SEASCAPES 52

Chapter Eight GLORIOUS GARDENS 56

Chapter Nine TANTALIZING TROPICS 62

Chapter Ten WONDERFUL WILDERNESS 68

Chapter Eleven MAJESTIC MOUNTAINS 75

Chapter Twelve FINE FINISHING TECHNIQUES 80

AUTHOR'S POSTSCRIPT 93

BIBLIOGRAPHY 93

RESOURCES 94

ABOUT THE AUTHOR 95

INDEX 96

INTRODUCTION

Drawing on my life-long love of nature, the last several years have been spent on a journey, an exploration of a new path in my quilting life. I am enamored with landscape quilts and have spent this time perfecting my skills in this art form. This road of creativity has had many unexpected twists and turns, and the countless discoveries made along the way have led me to become a better quiltmaker. This book shows you how to make landscape quilts using my simple, non-threatening techniques. With this book as a guide, I teach quiltmakers of all levels to design and complete a landscape quilt, from inception to completion.

Although some landscape artists copy, trace, and enlarge their design sources and use them as a pattern, I do not. I much prefer the spontaneity of designing without the benefit or constraints of a pattern. I do, however, enlarge and trace selected design elements, such as structures, to get the correct perspective.

The key element when beginning a landscape quilt is selecting an appropriate design inspiration. Your first project should be a simple design without excess detail, giving you the opportunity to create and finish a project and feel proud of your efforts. Depending on your design, a good size for your first quilt is approximately 26" by 20". Don't start too small, as miniatures are more difficult. Making a large landscape quilt for your first project isn't advisable either, as you should enjoy yourself without becoming overwhelmed. The projects in Chapter Six, *Luscious Little Landscapes*, are suitable for beginning quilters.

In addition to my quilts, many talented landscape artists and students generously showcase their spectacular landscape quilts in this book. Most of these artists use methods similar to mine and share their inspirations, techniques, tips, and processes. There are ten projects in this book including instructions, yardage requirements, and techniques.

Beautiful inspirations from nature act as a catalyst for creativity. The scenic photographs included in this book provide the impetus you need to begin your landscape quilts. I hope these photographs inspire you to stretch, grow, and challenge yourself to new levels. If you own a camera, carry it with you at all times so you can take photos for your design inspiration.

Giving myself permission to play and explore uncharted pathways has been the biggest step I have taken in my quiltmaking adventures, and I encourage you to do the same. When trying to impart a realistic interpretation in nature, it is sometimes necessary to invent methods to reach your goals. Before attempting a landscape quilt, give yourself permission to take risks, to play, to succeed, and to enjoy the journey. Creating a landscape quilt using my techniques should be fun!

When embarking on a landscape quilt, I study my inspiration as though I am looking through the lens of a camera. Most often, I use a photograph, a picture in a magazine or book, a catalog, a greeting card, or calendar as my inspiration. In this book, I give you the techniques to create your own masterpiece. Don't be alarmed when I break the rules and encourage you to do likewise! If you are unsure of yourself, use one of the projects provided for an initial trial run, or try a beginning quilt as featured in Chapter Six. After you complete your first quilt, spread your wings and fly, designing and creating an original landscape quilt using the techniques shared in this book.

As most quilt jurors or judges will share with you, fine finishing techniques in quiltmaking are just as important as the design. When completed, a landscape quilt needs to hang flat and square and be treated as a piece of valuable artwork for display on the wall. A gifted artist featured in this book, Sonia Grasvik, shares her remarkable methods to accomplish these tasks.

More than anything, I want you to succeed. My greatest reward is when you discover a newfound capacity for creativity. When your work exceeds your greatest expectations, I am ecstatic!

Joyce R. Becker

TOOLS OF THE TRADE

Most quilters already have many of the tools necessary to create a landscape quilt. There are a few tools that are essential when creating a landscape using my method. I suggest you buy what you don't have to avoid frustration later on. The following is a list of tools I recommend.

A sewing machine with the capability of lowering the feed dogs (which "feed" the fabric through the machine) for free-motion stitching. Students often show up at my workshops saying, "Can't I just put tape over my feed dogs?" Well, yes, you can, but it's not quite the same. Most of the techniques I use are done with the feed dogs dropped, including: attaching the elements such as trees or flowers, extensive machine embroidery, and machine quilting. Before purchasing my current sewing machine, I had a sewing machine with feed dogs that could not be lowered, and the only stitch choices were a zigzag and straight stitch. I used to tell myself, "It'll do." Boy, was I wrong! Once I purchased a machine that allowed me to explore new techniques, my creativity took off and hasn't slowed down since. You don't have to have the most expensive machine on the market with all of the gadgets. As long as the feed dogs on your sewing machine can be dropped, you have the ability to do free-motion stitching, and straight and zigzag stitches are available, you have all that is required from a machine for creating landscape quilts using my methods.

A darning/free-motion foot. A spring-loaded darning foot allows you to move and control the fabric instead of the machine moving or feeding the fabric. The darning foot is necessary if you plan to make a landscape quilt using my methods. Some darning feet come with a very small opening. If you have the option of purchasing a darning foot with a larger opening, do so. It is easier to see where you are going and where you have been when using the foot with the larger opening.

An open-toe embroidery foot. Although it is not crucial, I find an open-toe embroidery foot is helpful when attaching large elements to my landscape quilts. I use an open-toe embroidery foot in combination with a satin or zigzag stitch with matching or invisible thread to attach structures, such as a lighthouse, a building, or a wall.

A ¼" foot. This foot is helpful when attaching mitered borders (page 83).

A walking foot. The walking foot is useful for straight-line quilting, and for attaching the binding. The walking foot feeds the top of the quilt at the same pace as the bottom goes through the feed dogs. Your quilt won't bunch or pucker underneath.

Darning or free-motion foot

¼" foot

Open-toe embroidery foot

Sewing machine feet

Sewing machine table extension. Stitching landscape quilts without a table extension can be very difficult. The table extensions sold with most machines are adequate at best. I suggest either buying or building an acrylic extension table to increase the surface to hold the quilt while you stitch. My husband and a friend made my table extension from an acrylic desktop protector. They drilled out a hole for the arm with a high-speed drill, and glued on wooden legs purchased at a home improvement store.

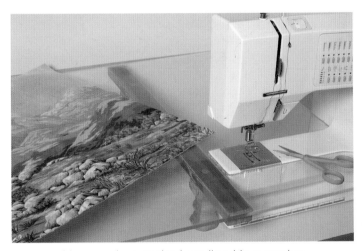

Homemade, over-sized acrylic table extension

Starch. Starch is the single most important product in my process. When cutting out elements such as leaves, flowers, grass, and so on, the heavier the starch, the easier the cutting. See Chapter Three for specifics.

Scissors. I recommend razor-sharp scissors with cushion grip handles, specifically designed to reduce the amount of pressure on your hand from frequent use. Cutting instructions and samples are in Chapter Three. See Resources.

Spray glue. My techniques involve a great deal of gluing. Having tried most glues and glue sticks on the market, I prefer spray adhesive. See Chapter Three for gluing techniques.

Spray adhesive

Scissors

Spray starch

Lightweight fusible interfacing (also known as Vilene). Stabilizing the back of your canvas with Pellon lightweight or sheer fusible interfacing is essential when using my techniques. Stabilizing your canvas first prevents your landscape quilt from puckering, moving out of shape, or being sucked down into the feed dogs while stitching. Tear-away stabilizers do not work well in this medium. Stabilizing techniques will be discussed later in this chapter.

Cutting mat, ruler, and rotary cutter. Rotary tools are necessary, especially to square up your design. Purchase a large cutting mat, a 24" x 6" ruler, and a large and a small rotary cutter. Large square rulers are especially helpful when squaring up your landscape quilt.

Rotary tools

Extra bobbin case. You will be adjusting the tension on your bobbin case frequently, so it is worth spending the extra money for a second bobbin case. Save your original bobbin case for regular sewing, and adjust the tension only on the extra bobbin case. I marked my extra case with nail polish, and I keep extra screws on hand because once a screw is dropped, it is almost impossible to locate.

Sewing machine needles. I recommend a wide variety of sewing machine needles because my landscape quilts include extensive machine embroidery and quilting with a wide variety of specialty threads. The needles are listed in order of my preference:

75/11 or 90/14 Embroidery needles (red dot) for machine embroidery and machine quilting

80/12 or 100/18 Topstitch needles for stitching through thick layers

80/12 Metallica for specialty or metallic threads

I occasionally use Jeans needles for extremely thick surfaces or when using a thick thread.

Bobbin case and needles

Thread. I use a large variety of thread in my landscape quilts. In order to make landscape quilts using my techniques, you will need invisible thread; I use clear or smoke nylon thread. Lightweight bobbin thread or lingerie thread are both good choices for bobbin thread; these come in a limited number of colors. Stock up on a variety of cotton, rayon, and machine embroidery threads. See Chapter Five for additional thread recommendations.

Bobbin thread

Batting. I recommend low-loft batting. It is easy to manipulate while machine quilting and lies flat, which is important since wall quilts should appear flat on the wall, like a piece of art.

Gizmos and gadgets. Each of us has our favorite little tools that we use to make our sewing lives easier. Some of my favorites include:

A reducing glass. A reducing glass helps you take in the entire project and makes your in-progress design appear finished. Another option is a "keyhole," which is available at most home improvement centers.

Bamboo skewers. Bamboo skewers allow you to hold down unstitched elements and stitch near or over the skewer without breaking a needle. I much prefer a bamboo skewer to a metal stiletto.

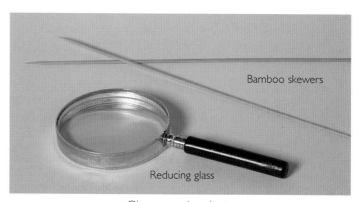

Bamboo skewers

Reducing glass

Gizmos and gadgets

Other Essentials

Fabric markers, artist pencils, and textile paint. I frequently use dye pens, fabric markers, artist's pencils, and textile paint to enhance my designs. These tools are used primarily to shade, augment, or add depth to elements in a landscape quilt. See Chapter Four for painting techniques. (See Resources for paints and pencils.)

Fabric markers, pencils, and textile paints

Fusible web or bonding agent. I use two-sided pressure-sensitive web for bonding two layers of fabric together for three-dimensional effects, or to bond large elements, such as structures, to my design. See Chapter Three for bonding examples.

Full-spectrum light. A good true-color light helps you reduce eyestrain while you design and stitch. I have a floor model with an optional magnifying glass. I use the magnifying glass to thread my machine needle, and for precision stitching. There are several models to choose from.

An office chair. You need a chair with good support while sewing. I use a standard office chair with wheels. I can stitch at my machine, turn around while still in my chair and iron from a sitting position, or design on my working wall, which is directly above my ironing board, all without getting up.

Organized fabric. Having your fabric separated by color and elements helps save time. I have a 6' x 6' bookcase with fifteen slots for fabric storage. My fabric is separated by elements such as flowers, leaves, rocks, trees, bricks, water, and so on. Having your fabric organized allows you to pick up a stack of fabric and quickly choose what you need for a particular project.

Trees

Rocks

Grasses

Flowers

Fabric sorted by theme

Camera. Taking photos of your in-progress work is helpful. It is difficult to assess your own work, but photographs don't lie. If your design isn't working, the values are incorrect, or your borders are too strong, a photograph will show you. I use an instant camera to give me quick snapshots. I also keep a digital camera and a 35mm camera in my studio to make prints and slides of my in-progress and completed quilts.

CREATING A MUSLIN CANVAS

Read through this book before selecting your first project. You need to determine the approximate measurements for your landscape. Then it is time to create a canvas. Building your design on a canvas backed with a stabilizer allows you to design your quilt from the top down and gives you a method for designing directly on the wall. A canvas is most often a piece of bleached or unbleached muslin cut a few inches larger than the desired finished size of your landscape quilt. Having an extra few inches around the perimeter of your canvas makes it easier to square your design without losing important elements. If you use a single background fabric, such as in *Fall*, the background fabric can also act as your "canvas," but it too must be stabilized.

1. Using your rotary tools, cut a piece of muslin that is approximately 3" larger all around than the finished quilt.

2. Press muslin with steam until all wrinkles and puckers disappear.

Using a single background fabric as a canvas, *Fall* by Joyce R. Becker

Stabilizing Your Canvas

Stabilizing your canvas with a lightweight fusible interfacing prevents the canvas from shrinking, moving out of shape, puckering, or being sucked down into the feed dogs while you stitch. Having tried every stabilizer on the market, I prefer lightweight or sheer interfacing. This interfacing gives your landscape canvas just enough stability to accommodate the extensive thread work required without adding bulk or making your quilt stiff.

1. Preheat your iron to a low or medium-low (rayon) setting with steam.

2. Cut the fusible interfacing the same size as your canvas.

If your canvas is large, overlap two or more pieces of fusible interfacing.

3. Place the bubble (rough) side of the interfacing on the back of your canvas.

4. Before fusing, place the canvas muslin side up on your ironing board. Check to see if any of the stabilizer extends beyond the edges of the muslin canvas. You risk getting your iron mucked up with adhesive unless you cut accurately or use a pressing cloth.

5. Press with steam. If the stabilizer doesn't adhere, slightly raise the temperature of your iron.

tip

If your iron is too hot, the stabilizer will bubble up, wrinkle, and not lie flat. It is possible to reposition and reuse the puckered stabilizer by peeling it away from the canvas. Smooth and reposition the stabilizer, and lower the temperature on your iron before you press again.

A WORKING OR DESIGN WALL

A working wall is crucial when designing landscape quilts. It very difficult to design a landscape quilt on the floor or flat on a table. Your design wall can be a portable working surface or a permanent fixture in your sewing room or studio. Creating the right perspective in your landscape quilt is crucial and cannot be accomplished unless you design on the wall. Working walls are simple to make regardless of your space constraints.

Inexpensive Working Walls

If you don't have a lot of room in your home or you need a portable design wall, there are several options:

1. A flannel-backed vinyl tablecloth can serve as your design wall. Secure the top of the tablecloth, flannel side out, to a closet door or an empty wall in your home.

2. A piece of batting or flannel cut a few inches larger than your design can serve as your working wall. Again, secure to a closet door or wall.

tip

If you work close to a door or open window, tape or pin down all of the edges of your working wall so design elements don't blow off.

3. A foam-core board, available at most craft supply stores, is another option for an inexpensive, portable working wall. Foamcore comes in many sizes and will accommodate most small- to medium-sized landscape projects. You can pin directly into the foamcore and it can be used repeatedly.

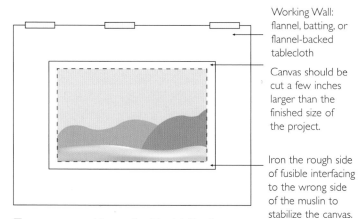

Working Wall: flannel, batting, or flannel-backed tablecloth

Canvas should be cut a few inches larger than the finished size of the project.

Iron the rough side of fusible interfacing to the wrong side of the muslin to stabilize the canvas.

Temporary working wall with stabilized canvas

Permanent Design Walls

There are several materials appropriate for permanent design walls. Home insulation board, available at most home improvement centers, is one option for a permanent design wall. The materials for my design wall were purchased at a home improvement surplus store and were originally used as dividers. My husband butted together three panels and secured them directly onto my studio wall with bolts. Since the yucky gold color of the panels was not suitable for photographing my quilts, I covered the panels with white batting, and secured the batting with staples.

Chapter Two SELECT A DESIGN INSPIRATION

SIMPLICITY IS KEY

Inspiration needs to have one thing: simplicity. If you choose a design with too many elements, especially the first time around, you may become discouraged and relegate your landscape quilt to the back of the closet. For example, if I find a photograph with a captivating scene I want to translate into a landscape quilt but the design is too complex, I simplify the photograph by eliminating elements that seem unnecessary or are distracting.

Sometimes I place a frame, such as those used for matting a photograph, over my inspirational photograph. I move the frame across the entire photograph, auditioning the areas to keep or eliminate.

Consider the panoramic photograph below on the left.

This photograph is stunning, and when simplified by cropping, still has all the major elements to make it a successful design option for a landscape quilt.

A panoramic scene to use as a design inspiration

Simplifying a design inspiration

WHAT TO LOOK FOR IN A DESIGN

When contemplating a new design inspiration there are several items to consider. What will be the focal point in your landscape? Will your design be balanced? Will you be able to translate the perspective through your fabric selection? Although I have no formal art background, I study paintings, art books, photography books, and nature itself so I am able to translate my fiber art into realistic portrayals. Most of the time, the focal point in my design will be off center, with another design element on the opposite side for balance. As I stated, when I'm beginning a landscape quilt, I study my inspiration as though I am looking through the lens of a camera, framing the most advantageous view, as a photographer would do.

Another important consideration when selecting a photograph or design inspiration is to look for a design that is interesting from different distances. Perhaps the mountains in the background are subtle, while the water in the middle portion of the quilt is colorful with movement, and the elements in the foreground, such as bushes or flowers, add another texture and dimension. A landscape quilt should pique your interest from far away and close up. It should beckon you to come and look closer. Decorative stitching, painting, fusing or bonding, and other surface design techniques can make your quilt more interesting, stimulating the visual juices. Aren't you drawn to those quilts at quilt exhibits that have a strong visual impact? Think about visual impact as you design your landscape quilt.

Negative Space

When I first began making landscape quilts, I didn't take into consideration that my art might be too busy or too stimulating. In some cases, there was nowhere for the eye to rest. Now, I try to leave negative space, or empty places, so the eye can rest on the focal point and then move outward over the body of the rest of the quilt.

New Zealand Adventure is restful because your eye goes to the subtlety of the mountains, broadens to the ocean, and finally moves to the foreground. There is a great deal of negative space, yet the quilt offers interest on different levels. It is pleasing to look at from far away, yet as you get closer, you can see and almost feel the activity of the water breaking on the shore. Moving

Using negative space in a landscape quilt, *New Zealand Adventure* by Joyce R. Becker

closer, you notice the foliage in the foreground and the extensive threadwork or perhaps the textile painting and other surface design elements of the water. Spend some time thinking about your design before you begin; consider incorporating some negative space into your landscape quilt.

tip

If you use a copyrighted image for your inspiration and plan on exhibiting or publishing your quilt, it is necessary to obtain permission from the copyright owner.

SELECTING FABRICS

With any quilting project, selecting and purchasing the fabric is half the fun! What's really exciting is that fabric designers and manufacturers have realized the demand for fabrics that are appropriate for landscape quilts and are producing these fabrics for us. Selecting fabrics for your landscape quilt should be easy, once you understand what to look for. The wide varieties of fabrics I include are good examples of the types that work best in landscapes. If you study the samples in this chapter, and the fabrics used in the quilts in this book, you'll be better prepared when you shop for fabrics suitable for landscape quilts.

What to Look for

Solids don't work! Students often show up for my workshops with solid fabrics versus prints. Solid fabrics are flat and static and give no suggestion of texture, depth, or perspective. When shopping for fabrics, look for prints that have more than one value. Different values in fabric give more interest and add realism. Batik fabrics often have several values that can imply movement or texture.

Background Fabric

The most important fabric you will purchase for your landscape quilt is the background. The background fabric sets the tone, mood, and feel of your whole quilt. Study your design inspiration before you shop for your background fabric. Keep in mind that value is more important than color. Good choices for background fabrics include:

1. Hand-painted and batik fabrics.

2. Commercial hand-dyed fabrics (see Resources).

Realism

When shopping for fabric for particular elements in my landscape quilt, my eye always goes to the fabrics that are most realistic. If my landscape quilt includes foliage, for example, I shop for foliage prints that are natural in appearance.

What if you find a fabric that is realistic but the scale is too large or the color is wrong? No problem, buy it anyway. Some elements in nature, such as a leaf, a plant, or a flower, can be cut down to the appropriate scale and the color can be changed with fabric pens. Chapter Three demonstrates trimming and shaping, and Chapter Four discusses the use of fabric pens.

Fabric Value

Value is not a complicated term. Value simply means light, medium, dark, and everything in-between. Value has nothing to do with color. A dark blue or dark green fabric often *reads* the same value as black from a distance. When selecting fabrics for landscape quilts, value is always more important than color. If I am creating a mountain scene, the mountains that are farthest away have the lightest value. I will often use the reverse side of a fabric for the row of mountains that is furthest back, and the right side of that fabric for the row of mountains that come next. The next closer row of mountains can be a different color, as long as the value is correct. The mountains in *New Zealand Adventure* illustrate this point.

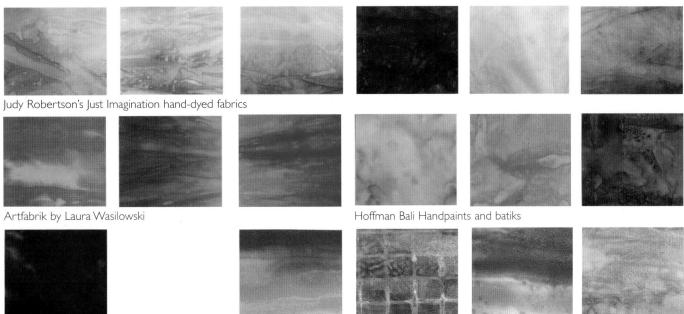

Judy Robertson's Just Imagination hand-dyed fabrics

Artfabrik by Laura Wasilowski

Hoffman Bali Handpaints and batiks

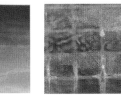

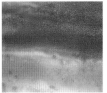

Hoffman Bali Handpaints and batiks

Mickey Lawler's SkyDyes hand-painted fabrics

Samples of background fabrics

SkyDye painted fabrics

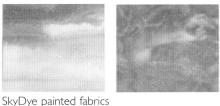

Notice how value, not color, suggests perspective and distance in this landscape quilt. The mountains furthest away are a different color than the mountains closer to the foreground but the value is correct. Always keep value, not color, in mind when shopping for landscape fabrics. When in doubt, use a value finder tool, available at most quilt shops, to check fabric values.

Value is more important than color as demonstrated in *New Zealand Adventure.*

Fabric Scale

Another important factor to take into consideration when shopping for landscape fabrics is the scale of the print. Scale can make or break your design. If you find a commercial tree fabric but the preprinted tree is just too small, you'll need to keep shopping or create your own tree. Flowers, leaves, grasses, rocks, and other elements that are preprinted can be trimmed down to the correct scale, while other elements, such as foliage, trees, and mountains, cannot. Cutting techniques are demonstrated in Chapter Three. Always keep scale in mind when shopping for landscape fabrics.

Preprinted Elements

Fabric designers have produced whole lines of wonderful fabrics with preprinted clouds, mountains, colorful skies, rocks, bricks, walls, and many other elements of nature. The Material Resources fabric line by Julie Golimowski has a wonderful array of fabrics suitable for landscape quilts. Julie's line includes both architectural and landscape fabrics, including: roofs, bricks, plaster walls, rocks, boulders, grasses, foliage, and so on (see Resources).

Preprinted fabrics are wonderful choices to include in your landscape quilts because they accomplish much of the work for you. Always reach for the fabrics that portray realism versus those fabrics that are "too patterned" or have regularly repeating motifs and patterns. Although beautiful, impressionistic designed fabrics most often don't work in landscape quilts. The printed areas are not well-defined and become blurred when viewed from a distance.

Preprinted fabrics from the Material Resources fabric line

Shop for fabrics with definite or hard-line edges. Fabrics with soft designs or edges blend together in your design, offering little definition between design elements.

Impressionistic fabric and fabric with a repeating pattern

Fabrics that don't work in landscape quilts

Visual Interest

Although our natural "quilting impulse" is to try and match everything when creating a quilt, the opposite is true when creating a landscape quilt. In order to convey perspective, realism, and visual interest in your landscape quilts my advice is simple: study nature. Look out the window and really see! Go out with fresh eyes. Are the trees the same height? Are the colors of the leaves on the foliage all the same green? Do the flowers all point in the same direction and are they formed the same? Trees are usually different heights. Some may appear perfect while others slant or have branches that stick out at odd angles. Depending on the exposure of the sun, two trees standing next to one another can be different values. Perhaps one tree is in full sun while the other tree is in partial shade. The same holds true for leaves and foliage. The foliage closest to the ground or the underside of a leaf is usually darker, while those elements in the sunlight are lighter in value. Flowers are never exactly alike in color or size. Some flowers might be in the bud stage, or slightly open, while others face different directions. Other flowers might be partially hidden or covered with leaves, exposing only a portion of the flower.

Incorporating differences and variety in your landscape quilts increases visual interest. When shopping for "leaf"

fabric, for example, look for a variety of commercial prints. It doesn't matter if the fabrics differ in color or value; in fact, it's better if they do! In my quilt, *Morning Glories Climbing Over the Gate*, notice the wide variety of leaves. The variety in leaf type, size, value, and color adds visual interest and makes the quilt realistic. Now take a look at the flowers. Compared to leaves in the quilt, you'll notice the number of flowers is considerably lower.

Incorporating visual interest using a variety of leaves and flowers, *Morning Glories Climbing Over the Gate* by Joyce R. Becker

When making garden quilts, our urge is to include an overabundance of flowers and not enough leaves or foliage. Next time you are standing in a garden, look around and actually study the ratio of leaves and foliage to the number of flowers. You'll be surprised!

Take your design inspiration with you when shopping for fabric; it will provide valuable visual clues. Having a visual impression of how things look in nature while shopping for landscape fabrics is very important.

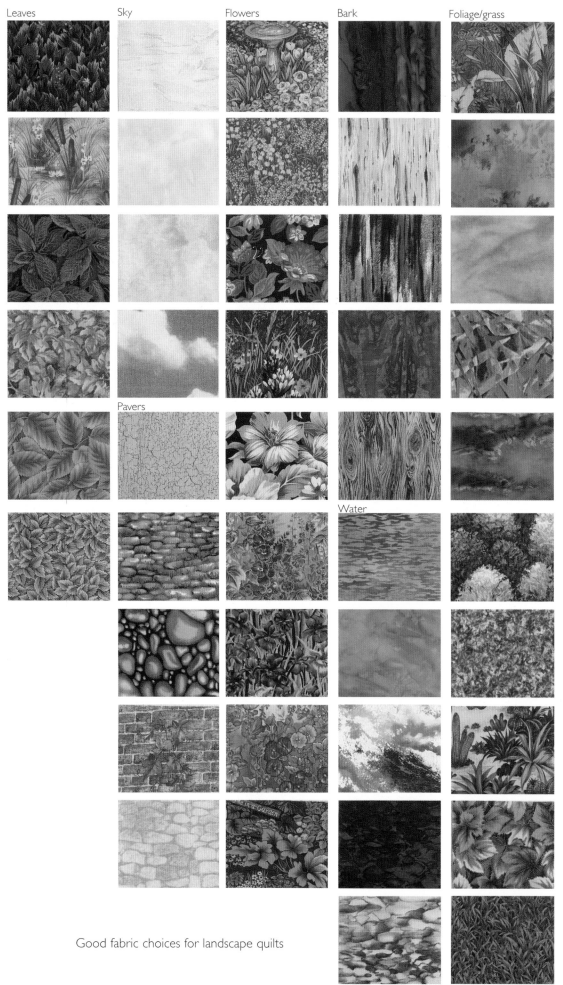

Leaves   Sky   Flowers   Bark   Foliage/grass

Pavers

Water

Good fabric choices for landscape quilts

Perspective

Perspective is the most difficult element to achieve in landscape quilts. There are many ways to accomplish perspective in your quilts through the use of fabric and other surface design methods. As I discussed earlier, use the wrong side of a certain fabric to portray distant features, and the right side of the fabric as you move to the foreground in your scene. This is an effective method of using value and definition to achieve perspective in your landscape quilt.

I frequently use overlays to help define perspective. Shading with the appropriate values of tulle, netting, or organza accomplishes realistic perspective with little work. For example, when I created *New Zealand Adventure* (page 75) my goal was to use only fabrics that I had in my stash. The fabric I had on hand for the sky was much too strong in value, but was otherwise perfect. By placing three layers of white polyester organza over my sky fabric, the sky fabric then mirrored the value in my photographic inspiration. The same objective was accomplished with the mountain fabrics, except this time I used tulle as an overlay on the mountains where the value was too strong.

Samples of tulle, netting, and organza to use for overlays

Texture

Think about texture in nature and how to add it to your landscape quilts. What do I mean by texture? Look at the bark on trees, the rough surface of a large boulder, or the fuzzy center of some flowers. You almost always want to touch these textured surfaces just to see how they feel.

Incorporating and translating texture into your landscape quilts adds an important ingredient, and sometimes, another dimension to your project. When I created the trees in my quilt *I Will Lift Up Mine Eyes Unto the Hills* (page 78), I wanted the bark to look real. I used my computer and searched for specific types of bark on the Internet, then enlarged this image and printed it in color. Having a visual clue while I shopped for suitable fabric helped me with my fabric choice. I later added extensive machine embroidery with colored threads to add more texture, making the trees appear realistic (see Chapter Five for machine embroidery tips).

Tree bark detail

Making Fabric Work for You

Thinking about fabric in a new way to make it work for you to achieve perspective, value, texture, and realism is your goal. You can incorporate painting, sponging, thread-work, overlays, or all of the above. Don't pass up a fabric until you think about what you can do with it. Chapters Four and Five offer tips on how to incorporate different techniques to make your commercially purchased fabrics realistic. Look at the photographs of the quilts and notice how the artists have altered certain fabrics to convey realism, depth, texture, and perspective.

When you shop for fabrics, instead of looking at the big picture think about how a certain element in a fabric can be used in your landscape quilts. Don't reject a bolt of fabric, for example, that has bunnies printed on it because you don't want the bunnies. Think about the wonderful, realistic foliage surrounding the bunnies and how you can incorporate that portion of the fabric into a landscape. If a fabric is perfect except for a value that is too strong, look at the wrong side of the fabric, or think about a layer of tulle, netting, or polyester organza to tone down the value. There are wonderful fabrics available to make landscape quilts. It's up to you to utilize these fabrics and make them work in your landscape quilts.

I HAVE MY INSPIRATION, BUT HOW DO I BEGIN?

tip

For your first landscape project you will probably want to start with a smaller size quilt, approximately 26" x 20". Refer to Luscious Little Landscapes, Chapter Six, for project ideas.

Starch, Starch, and More Starch

Before beginning the design process, prepare your fabric. All fabric that will be cut into pieces needs to be heavily starched. Limp fabric is incredibly difficult to cut.

1. Use heavy-or medium-weight spray starch.

2. Starch ¼ yard or less of each fabric.

3. Starch **both sides** of your fabric heavily and press with a dry iron.

4. You've starched enough when the fabric stands up by itself!

Design Placement and Guidelines

You have your design inspiration and your canvas is in place on your working wall. Now comes the fun part: designing your landscape quilt.

tip

Make a color copy and, if necessary, enlarge your design. Enlarging your inspirational source makes the design details clearer, and the design process easier. Fold this copy into thirds, horizontally. The folded lines are placement guides to help you determine where to place your fabrics.

Background Placement

1. Fold your canvas into thirds horizontally. Lightly mark the folds with a pencil to create placement guides. The first thing you will place on your canvas is your background, such as your sky fabric.

2. Using your enlarged inspiration as a guide, determine the size of the background in the design. If your enlarged inspiration has sky that extends to the second fold, then you need to cut enough sky fabric to extend just beyond the second fold on your canvas. Measure the distance from the top of your canvas to the second fold on your canvas and add ½" to the measurement, then cut the fabric to that size.

Placement line

Placement line

Copy and enlarge design inspiration with horizontal placement lines.

3. Pin the background fabric into place on your canvas.

4. Refer to Chapter Four for basting instructions. Sew ¼" away from the outside edge of your background fabric, using invisible thread in the top and lightweight thread in your bobbin.

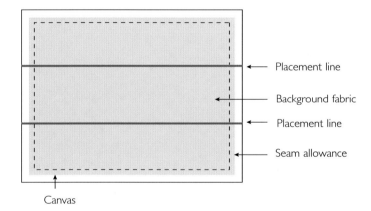

Placement line

Background fabric

Placement line

Seam allowance

Canvas

Baste the background fabric to the canvas using invisible thread.

5. Stand back from your canvas and check to make sure the value of your background fabric is correct. If the value is too strong, recommendations follow for correcting it or toning it down.

Audition the Feature Fabrics

1. Pin your fabrics onto your working wall in their approximate location in the design.

2. Step back and look at your fabrics through a reducing glass or keyhole.

3. Fabrics with unsuitable values or colors will usually jump out as if saying, "I don't belong here, take me out!"

4. Continue auditioning fabrics until you feel the design and textures mix and the values work well together.

Value and Perspective

If the value of your background fabric is too strong, applying overlays of tulle or polyester organza may help mute or tone down the value. Keep ½ yard amounts of fine tulle or netting on hand in a variety of colors just for this purpose. Sometimes, one layer of white tulle will do the trick; other times you might require several layers of tulle. You can also layer different colors of tulle or netting to reach the desired effect.

Audition the overlays by positioning and pinning them onto your background fabric on the design wall. If the value of your background fabric is much too strong, overlays of polyester organza may solve the problem.

Pin, then stitch the overlays to the background using invisible thread. Stitch as close as possible to the edges, and trim with scissors.

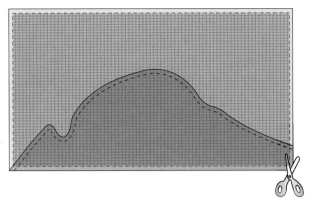

Baste and trim tulle, netting, or organza overlays.

tip

To create a subtle effect of perspective (lighter in the distance, darker in the foreground) layer tulle over part of the background fabric, leaving the background fabric closest to the foreground without an overlay. Using layers of overlays, you can portray fog, filtered sunlight, or other moods in your landscape quilts.

tip

Avoid using fabric adhesives on most overlay fabrics; they leave a sticky residue.

Attaching Foreground Elements

In most designs, the next step is to attach your foreground. If you are working on an ocean scene, after the sky is in place the water is the next fabric to place on your canvas. Think through your design as if it were a typical appliqué project. Fabrics need to be added in a logical order.

tip

Water, such as an ocean or a lake, must be horizontal. Your water line **must be straight** when you place it on canvas or your design will always look lopsided!

In-progress photographs of my quilt, *Winter Wonderland*, show the natural progression or order of a design. In this design, the background sky fabric was stitched onto the

Design process for *Winter Wonderland*, photograph by Joyce R. Becker

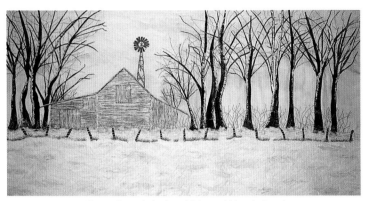

Completed design, *Winter Wonderland*

canvas first, followed by the snow fabrics. The trees, barn, and fence were glued onto the surface of the background fabrics, then stitched into place once the design was complete.

CUTTING SUGGESTIONS FOR DESIGN ELEMENTS

For the most part, if you cut with "reckless abandon," your landscape quilt will be more successful. Yes, there are elements in your design that require "fussy" or precision cutting, but for the most part, your challenge will be to cut like a six-year-old. As stated in Chapter One, using razor-sharp scissors makes cutting easier (see Resources).

How to Cut

tip

When cutting, move the fabric, not the scissors. If your fabric is heavily starched, moving the fabric gives you more control and makes cutting a breeze. Refer to your design inspiration as you cut.

1. Each element in nature is different and no two elements will be cut the same. Your goal is to achieve realism, so the shapes you cut need to convey how these elements appear in nature. Mountains, for example, are cut differently than background foliage. Use your photographic inspiration as your guide, keeping the correct scale in mind as you cut.

2. When creating a quilt with rows of mountains, begin with the row of mountains furthest back in your design inspiration. To determine how much fabric you will need for your first row of mountains, audition your fabric on your canvas to get a rough estimate of the length and width requirements. Cut a piece of prestarched mountain fabric slightly larger than the desired amount. If you are apprehensive, practice on a prestarched scrap fabric until you are comfortable with the method.

tip

Smaller pieces of starched fabric are easier to manipulate and control when cutting.

3. What if your design has no mountains, just foliage or another element? Follow the same advice and let your eye be your guide. In nature, foliage or bushes in the distance do not appear in a straight line or look alike. Your challenge is to cut out dips and crannies in your foliage fabric to create the natural appearance of foliage. Cutting examples for foliage follow.

4. Refer to your design inspiration. As you cut, try to look at your design inspiration, not at your hand. Cut your first row of mountains, imitating the curves and heights, moving the fabric, not the scissors. Remember, you are trying to imitate what you see. It doesn't have to be exact.

5. Pin the row of mountains onto your canvas at the desired location. Step back from your design wall and look at the first row of mountains to determine if the placement is correct. Do the mountains and the scale seem realistic? If not, make corrections or cut a new row of mountains.

tip

Remember to use your fabric to its fullest extent. If your fabric can be reversed, use the wrong side of the fabric for the row of mountains furthest back and the right side of the fabric for the next row of mountains.

tip

Avoid blunt edges on the elements you cut from fabric. Taper or round-off edges so they appear natural.

6. Rather than describing how to cut each individual element in nature, refer to the photographs of the landscape quilts and samples in this book to help you with your cutting decisions. Samples of suitable landscape fabrics are included in Chapters One and Two.

tip

Cutting requires patience and can be time consuming. Spending the extra time to add lots of detailed cutting will make your completed quilt more realistic.

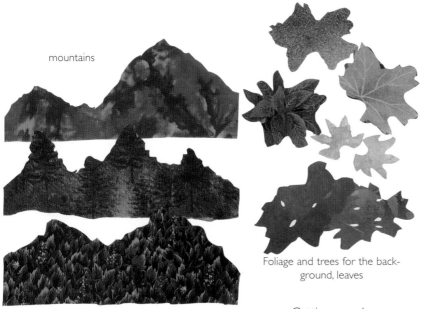

mountains

Foliage and trees for the background, leaves

Cutting samples

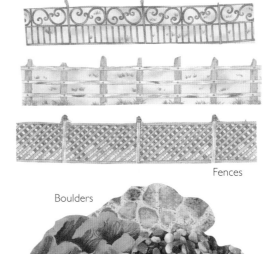

Fences

Boulders

Fussy Cutting

Certain elements in your design require "fussy" or precise cutting. Many commercial preprinted fabrics contain wonderful rocks, leaves, or flowers that you can incorporate into your designs.

1. Working with small pieces of prestarched fabric, cut the individual flowers, leaves, rocks, and so on out of the preprinted fabric. Cut precisely, following the printed shapes.

tip

If you know you will be fussy cutting certain fabrics in your landscape quilt, prestarch those fabrics and cut them out while you watch your favorite television programs. Keep a small wastebasket handy for scraps, and place the cut shapes into small bags sorted by elements.

2. The scale of your design changes, and elements in the foreground appear larger. If there is a field of flowers in your design, the scale of the flowers should grow larger as you move closer to the bottom edge of your quilt. Many fabrics accomplish this for you, other times you will have to cut fabric apart to achieve this goal. Notice in the photo how the scale of the flowers increases as you move closer to the foreground.

Fussy-cut floral fabric with increasing scale

Fussy cutting examples

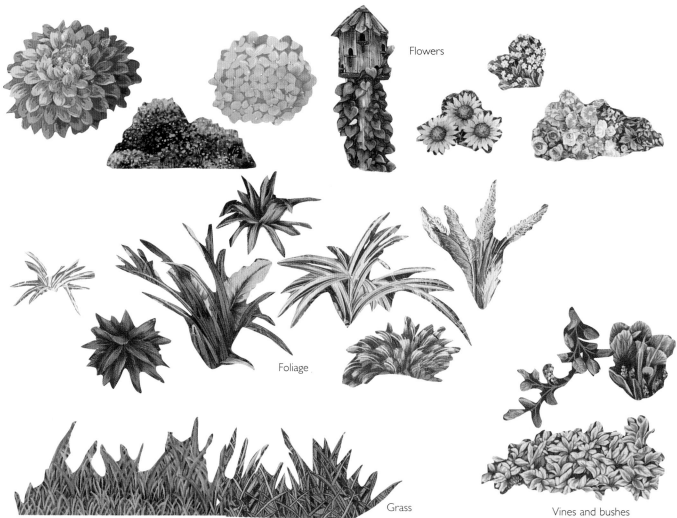

Flowers

Foliage

Grass

Vines and bushes

Creating Your Own Elements

Sometimes there are no preprinted elements available. No problem—accept the small challenge and create your own element.

1. After selecting a fabric to use for tree bark, your job is to recreate the specific tree in the correct scale for your landscape quilt. Use your eye to recreate the image portrayed on your design inspiration.

2. Use a small rotary cutter to cut out trees. Refer to your design inspiration to eyeball how large your tree needs to be. Cut out a tree from purchased bark or tree fabric. When cutting a tree, mimic the shape as it appears in your design inspiration. The trees in *Winter Wonderland* (page 68) look real because they twist and turn and are not straight up and down.

3. Don't throw away any scraps! They can be used for the branches and twigs on your trees. Refer to the samples provided and your photo inspiration for examples of size and position for your trees. Add roots or definition at the bottom of your tree when cutting.

4. Position your tree on your background fabric. When adding branches and twigs hide their edges under the trunk of the tree instead of butting the edges against the tree.

5. The same principles apply for boulders, rocks, or flower stems. Look for fabrics that capture the essence of the element, both in scale and value. Find a variety of fabrics that look like boulders or rocks, and cut out the elements in your design inspiration.

FUSIBLE WEB AND BONDING

There are times while creating a landscape quilt when it is easier to use a fusible bonding web instead of gluing. Large structures are much easier to position and place on your canvas when you use a fusible web.

The lighthouse in *Red Skies at Night, Sailor's Delight* (page 52) is an example of a structure that was fused into place.

Bonding Directions

1. Trace your structure on the web's paper lining.

2. Pull the paper liner off the other side of the fusible web and position it on the wrong side of the fabric.

3. Cut out the traced shape of your structure.

4. Remove the paper and place the structure on your canvas. The web is pressure sensitive and can be repositioned.

5. Fuse following manufacturer's instructions.

tip

If you have trouble removing the paper lining, score an X on the paper with a straight pin and pull the paper away from the web.

Flower stems and flower

Trees with branches and twigs

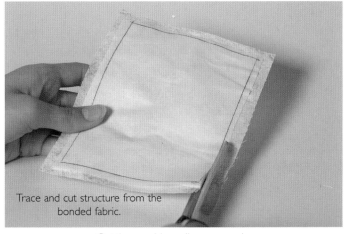

Trace and cut structure from the bonded fabric.

Cutting and bonding example

Boulders

Cutting recommendations

THREE-DIMENSIONAL ELEMENTS

Follow these instructions to create three-dimensional elements in your quilt, such as the leaves and flowers in *Morning Glories Climbing Over the Gate* (page 60).

1. Peel the paper off **both** sides of the fusible web.

2. Place the web between two similar pieces of fabric and press together with your hand.

3. Trim the edges of this fabric sandwich so none of the web extends beyond the edges.

4. Fuse the two fabrics together, using a pressing cloth, following the manufacturer's guidelines.

5. Cut out the individual shapes of leaves and flowers.

Instructions for stitching three-dimensional elements are included in Chapter Four.

tip

Other fabrics may be substituted for the underside of three-dimensional elements to create a specific effect. If you are cutting and bonding a leaf fabric and want the reverse side to appear darker for shading, select a fabric a shade darker in value for the back side of the leaf. If the printed element is too large, cut the shape smaller to fit your needs.

Front side of leaf

Back side of leaf using fabric with a darker value

GLUING

Attaching your elements with glue or adhesive is the next step in your process. As described in Chapter One, I prefer spray adhesives; you can also use glue sticks or a fabric adhesive of your choice. Remember to work in a well-ventilated area, and wear a dust mask.

Although you might be tempted to spray glue directly onto your canvas, I strongly advise against it. Spraying adhesive directly onto your canvas can result in a sticky surface, and the possibility of spotting. Follow these simple instructions for gluing.

1. Always "audition" a cut design element, such as a row of mountains, before attaching it to your canvas. As you become more comfortable with the design process, your eye will tell you if your positioning is correct.

2. Lay a piece of batting on your work surface for protection. Place the element to be glued wrong-side up on the batting. Spray or apply adhesive onto the fabric and place it onto the canvas.

tip

Elements that have been sprayed with glue and positioned on your canvas can be repositioned. Simply pull the element off the canvas, reapply adhesive, and reposition.

Batting with elements facing wrong-side up

How to glue

tip

As you build your design and move closer to the front or foreground, the values should become darker, as in nature.

MAKING CHANGES

You think your design is done, but something isn't quite right. What now? Do you pitch your quilt into a drawer with the rest of your UFOs and start over? No! There are ways to fix your design with minimum effort.

When a certain aspect of your design isn't working, don't worry, there's an easy solution. My philosophy is: If something isn't working, either cover it up, or cut it away and replace it. When I created *I Will Lift Up Mine Eyes Unto the Hills* (page 78) I changed the foreground three times before I was satisfied.

Covering Elements

Covering up undesirable elements, such as a foreground or water, is easy. Just build on top of what you already have. Select a new piece of fabric, audition it, and place the new fabric directly on top of the undesirable fabric. Glue or pin it into place.

tip

If you discover your error before the unsuitable fabric has been stitched down, pull it off and replace it.

Cutting Away Large Elements

It is perfectly acceptable to cut away portions of your quilt. I do it all the time! If a portion of your design just isn't working and you are too far along in the design process to cover it up, just cut away the undesirable portion. Before you throw up your hands and cry, "But my quilt is ruined," think again. My methodology is, after all, cutting apart and pasting stuff onto the surface of your quilt. Follow these instructions for cutting away portions of your quilt you are not happy with.

1. Cut away the undesirable portion.

2. Replace it with a more suitable fabric and glue or pin it into place.

3. Patch the back of the quilt with a piece of stabilized muslin large enough to cover the area that was replaced.

4. Sew the patch into place with invisible thread. Your problem is solved.

Repairing a mistake with a "patch"

Fixing Small Errors

Small errors are easily repaired in landscape quilts by substituting fabric with the appropriate value and scale. After completing my design for *Sanctuary* (page 61), I was unhappy with some of the flowers. The scale was off and the value too light. I found another floral fabric in the correct scale and value and simply covered the "offending" flowers.

Balance

What if your design doesn't appear balanced? Another simple solution: Add another element of interest to balance your design. I added the tree and chair pictured in my quilt, *Sanctuary*, after the fact, for balance.

PHOTOGRAPHING YOUR QUILT

You are finished with your basic design and are thrilled with the results. Before proceeding to the next chapter, where you learn how to attach elements, take a photograph. It will reveal things your eyes and mind won't! Sometimes we are just too close to our work to notice what is or isn't working. I keep a digital camera and an instant camera handy just for this purpose. Study the picture. Does your design appear balanced? Are the values correct? Are you happy with the result? If yes, you're ready to proceed. If not, make the necessary corrections.

tip

When your design is complete, leave it on the wall for a day or two. Do you need to change anything? Once you're satisfied with the design, move on to the next chapter.

Chapter Four BASTE AND EMBELLISH

This chapter deals with basting your design top using raw-edge appliqué, and adding design elements or embellishments for depth and texture.

BASTING USING RAW-EDGE APPLIQUÉ

Contrary to popular belief, raw-edge appliqué is totally acceptable. In some quilting circles, it is felt that raw-edge appliqué is second rate, and that edges need to be turned under. Using my methods, your landscape quilt will appear "finished" and the raw edges will not be seen when you complete your quilt. Students examining my quilts at very close range often exclaim, "I don't see any raw edges. Where are they?" I use many techniques to achieve this finished appearance. This chapter explains the basic instructions for attaching the elements in your landscape quilt using nylon invisible thread. You will be basting or stitching down the glued elements to your quilt top. Your quilts will look finished without the tell-tale signs of raw-edge appliqué quilts if you follow these techniques.

Stitching the Elements Onto Your Quilt Top

1. If you are working on a dark quilt use the smoke color thread, otherwise use the clear, light nylon thread.

2. Using a 75/11 embroidery needle, thread your machine according to the directions for your specific sewing machine.

tip

To reduce the risk of skipped stitches, some threads need to feed horizontally. Place a wide cup behind your machine and put the spool of thread into the cup so it feeds horizontally. You can also purchase adapters for your sewing machine for this purpose.

Thread is fed horizontally from a cup behind the sewing machine.

3. Fill your extra bobbin with lightweight bobbin thread in a neutral color. Some varieties only come in black or white, while other bobbin threads are available in several shades.

tip

If you want to keep the thread from twisting around the needle, put the thread through the last loop on your sewing machine after you thread the needle.

How to prevent twisted threads:

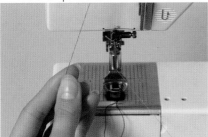

Step 1. Thread the needle.

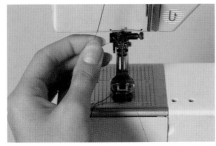

Step 2. Put the thread through the loop.

4. Before placing your bobbin into your machine, test to see if the tension on your bobbin is correct. Once your bobbin is loaded, pull out a couple of inches of thread. Now, holding your bobbin case by the thread with one hand, watch what happens. If your suspended bobbin "walks," or moves down by itself slowly, the tension on your bobbin is correct. If the bobbin falls suddenly, the tension on your bobbin is too loose. If nothing happens, the tension is too tight.

Test the bobbin tension by "walking" your bobbin.

The screw in your *extra* bobbin case (see Chapter One) may be turned in very small increments to adjust the tension. Turn the screw clockwise to tighten or counter-clockwise to loosen.

tip

Caution: Go slowly! If you loosen the screw in your bobbin case too much, it may fall out. The screw is tiny and almost impossible to find once it is dropped.

Keep your original bobbin case for other sewing projects where it is not necessary to adjust the tension.

5. If you find it difficult to thread the 75/11 sewing machine needle with the invisible thread, move up to a 90/14 needle. Remember that the larger the needle, the larger the hole in your quilt top, which may be visible.

tip

Mark the end of the invisible thread with a black pen. It makes threading a breeze!

6. If you want to make sure the bobbin thread doesn't show on the top, select a bobbin thread that blends with the color of your quilt top. If the tension of your bobbin thread and your top thread is adjusted correctly, there shouldn't be a problem with the bobbin thread "popping" to the front.

7. With the presser foot down, set the top tension on your machine. When using invisible or specialty threads I often stitch with my tension set on, or near, zero. However, each machine is different. When you stitch using a darning foot, your top tension needs to be very loose. Stitch width does not matter since you are free-motion stitching and controlling the stitch size as you sew.

tip

Adjust the top tension on your machine with the presser foot down; the mechanism on most machines does not engage until you take this step.

8. Once the thread tension is set, drop the feed dogs, and place the darning foot on your machine.

9. Pull the bobbin thread up by holding the top thread with your hand and rotating the flywheel on your sewing machine toward you with the other hand. The bobbin thread should pop up in a loop. Pull this loop until the free edge of the thread comes through. Make sure both the top thread and the bobbin thread are in the center of the darning foot. Use this method for all of the stitching techniques in your landscape quilts.

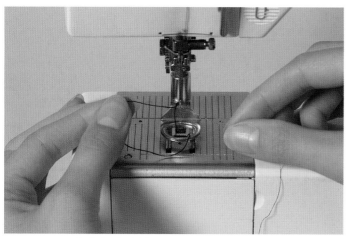

Pull the bobbin thread to the surface.

 tip

Always do a "test run" on a piece of stabilized fabric that is the same thickness as your quilt top to test both the top and bottom tensions.

10. If the top stitches are too loose on your test fabric, adjust the top tension. If the bobbin thread breaks, the tension is probably too tight. Loosen the tension slightly, a quarter turn at a time. Don't be afraid to adjust the bobbin tension on your extra bobbin case.

 tip

To adjust bobbin tension, turn the screw clockwise to make the tension tighter and counterclockwise to make it looser.

Each thread and each sewing machine is different, so it is impossible to make general recommendations regarding appropriate tension settings. Just give yourself permission to play with the tension adjustments on your machine until your stitches are even.

 tip

If your bobbin thread "pops up" or shows as dots on the front of your design, tighten your bobbin tension (clockwise), or thread the bobbin thread through the eye in the bobbin case arm (page 38). You may also consider replacing the bobbin thread with a coordinating or invisible thread.

11. Once you are satisfied with the tension settings, you are ready to begin basting the elements onto your canvas.

Stitching or Basting Sequence

Because you are working on a quilt top, not a sandwiched quilt, it is not necessary to baste the elements from the center out.

If your design has areas where the cut and glued elements are very small and you are concerned they might fall off, baste those first. Once those elements are basted, attach the remaining elements.

Basting the glued elements to your quilt top is not at all difficult. Keep in mind your goal is to anchor the cut and glued bits of fabric to the background, so the basting stitches should be minimal. Later, you will add more stitching with machine embroidery and machine quilting.

Place your landscape top into position for stitching. If you have a table extension or arm extension, use it. The more surface area you have to manipulate your quilt without disturbing the glued elements, the better. In addition to an over-sized acrylic table extension, my cutting table is directly behind my sewing machine, giving me a large area to manipulate my quilt while stitching.

Once your feed dogs are dropped, your darning foot is attached, and your needle is in down position, you are ready to roll!

1. Pull the bobbin thread to the top and take two or three stitches to anchor in place. Trim the threads.

2. Using a straight stitch, baste as close as possible to the outside edge of each element. If an element is really large, such as a structure or a large tree, stitch inside the element so it doesn't pucker later on.

 tip

Setting your machine in the needle-down position is a good habit. Your quilt will not move when you stop and start stitching, and you will not have any skipped stitches or broken thread.

3. Since you are only securing or basting the elements onto your quilt top, you can move from one element to the next without stopping. Invisible thread is undetectable and the stitching will not be apparent when your quilt is finished.

4. Stitch in a logical progression, moving from one area to the next.

Use invisible thread to baste or stitch the elements.

Complementing Your Design With Stitching

When attaching or basting elements to your quilt top, follow the natural shape of the element. Following the natural shape of an element makes the basting stitches less noticeable, enhancing the design. Use this same technique with your machine embroidery and machine quilting.

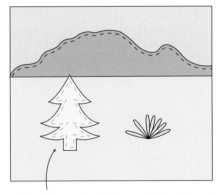

Sew along the natural shape of the elements.

Stitching Structures or Other Large Elements

When attaching structures or large elements to your quilt top, you may prefer to use a satin or zigzag stitch, which reduces the chance of shifting, instead of free-motion raw-edge appliqué. Match the thread color to the element or use invisible thread, depending on your preference. Follow these instructions to attach structures.

1. Attach an open-toe embroidery foot on your machine.

2. Feed dogs should be up, in the engaged position.

3. Use a lightweight bobbin thread, adjusting tension as described earlier in this chapter.

4. Thread the machine with a matching or invisible thread.

5. Set your stitch to zigzag.

6. Adjust the stitch width as desired. Set stitch length to satin stitch.

7. Use a scrap to see if you like the results. If not, make corrections.

8. With the needle down and your embroidery foot centered on the structure or element, begin stitching. Take two stitches forward and one backstitch to anchor. Trim your threads as you proceed. When turning corners, pivot so your corners line up with your presser foot and continue stitching until you come to the end of the element. Backstitch and trim threads.

tip

To assist with placement of the needle and the presser foot, place a large black dot with a permanent pen in the center of your open-toe machine embroidery foot. This dot helps you center your presser foot as you stitch.

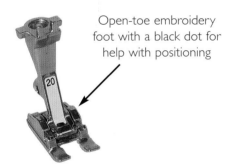

Open-toe embroidery foot with a black dot for help with positioning

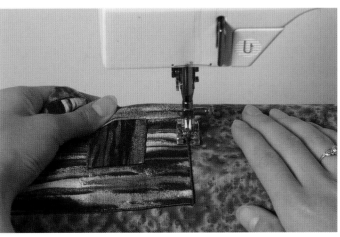

Satinstitch a structure into place.

PRESSING YOUR QUILT TOP

1. After your design is complete and the elements are basted with invisible thread, press your quilt **from the back** with heavy steam. You risk melting the invisible thread if you press from the front.

2. Use your hands to stretch the quilt top so any puckers disappear as you press.

3. If puckers still occur, snip a couple of the tight threads and press again.

Press your quilt top from the back with steam.

tip

If you plan on adding machine embroidery to your quilt top, press **after** you embroider.

TEMPTING TRICKS WITH PAINT, PENS, AND MORE

When creating landscape quilts, I sometimes use unusual methods to create realism. Most of these surface design embellishing techniques were created out of need. My philosophy is just go for it. Mistakes often lead to discovery.

Since landscape quilts are designed specifically to hang on the wall, you can include techniques that might seem questionable in more traditional quilts. There may come a time when you find it difficult to translate your vision into fabric because you aren't sure how to accomplish your goal.

When I can't come up with specific techniques to accomplish my objective, I put on my thinking cap. Sometimes, the answer appears in my dreams, or, in the case of *I Will Lift Up Mine Eyes Unto the Hills* (page 78), the answer came in the form of dryer lint when I did the laundry. Unhappy with the lack of realism and flat appearance of the original mountains, I struggled with a method to make the mountains appear natural, with contours. When I saw the dryer lint, I knew I had my answer. I placed the dryer lint on top of the mountains and molded the dryer lint into the shape I wanted. I covered the lint with a layer of fine tulle, matching or highlighting the value of the mountain.

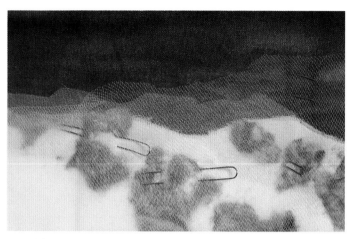

To add contour, layer dryer lint and overlay with tulle.

When you are struggling for a solution, think outside the box. When you make a mistake or something in your design isn't working, it forces you to find another pathway, sometimes with incredible results. After adding the surface design embellishing techniques included in this chapter, try the suggestions in Chapter Five for adding details and enhancing your design with machine embroidery.

Textile Paint

Textile paint gives you the opportunity to add details to your quilt with a minimum of work and can be used full strength or thinned with water, depending on your needs. Although textile paint does sit on the surface of your quilt, it isn't as stiff as you would expect.

Types of Textile Paint

As stated in Chapter One, I recommend many types of textile paints (see Resources).

Painting Supplies

1. High-quality artist brushes, foam brushes, and rollers. Most painting supplies may be ordered from a mail-order source (see Resources). Inexpensive foam brushes and rollers are available at most home improvement or craft stores.

tip

Artist brushes with long handles give you more control when painting.

2. Worktable. My worktable with folding legs was purchased at a discount store. Dips or scratches on the tabletop will imprint onto the fabric as you paint, so your worktable needs to be unblemished. To protect the top of your table, cover it with clear vinyl shelf liner instead of a plastic drop cloth because the surface will be smoother. Use a plastic drop cloth when you want to add texture by imprinting the fold lines and other imperfections into the fabric as you paint.

3. Latex gloves. Surgeon's gloves may be purchased in bulk at discount stores. Wear the gloves when applying textile paint, and remember to wear old clothes!

4. Damp rags and paper towels. Accidents often happen while you are painting. If you have damp rags nearby and you spill paint, you can blot or wash the paint off before it is too late.

5. Plastic drop cloth. Place a plastic drop cloth under your worktable—extending several inches beyond your work area—to provide protection for your floor.

6. Blow dryer and iron. After you finish painting, the paint needs to be dried and heat set. I have little patience and can't wait for my paint to cure naturally, so I dry my paint with a blow dryer and then heat set it from the back with a dry iron set on high. Follow the heat setting instructions provided in this chapter.

7. Old plastic margarine tubs, plastic disposable plates, kraft sticks, and plastic spoons. When mixing small amounts of textile paint with water, old plastic margarine tubs work well. Plastic disposable plates in a variety of sizes are another option. Save kraft sticks and old plastic spoons for mixing. Any of the plastic items used can be rinsed with hot water and soap and used again.

Creating Fabric With Textile Paint

1. When you cannot find a commercial fabric to suit your needs, create your own using textile paint. For example, in *Red Skies at Night, Sailor's Delight* (page 52)

I could not find a suitable commercial fabric for the water, so I painted the fabric with textile paint.

2. Use good quality white cotton sateen. Cotton sateen has a glow that shows through the paint and is especially nice for sky or water surfaces. Cotton sateen is available at some quilt shops or may be ordered on the Internet (see Resources).

3. Press the cotton sateen with steam so there are no wrinkles or puckers.

4. Place the pressed fabric on your worktable, stretching the fabric and securing it with masking tape or spring-loaded clamps, which are available at most home improvement stores.

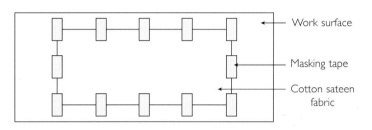

Work surface
Masking tape
Cotton sateen fabric

To prepare fabric for painting, slightly stretch and tape the fabric to a worktable.

5. If you are using textile paint from the jar, no color mixing is required.

6. For large applications, such as the water in *Red Skies at Night, Sailor's Delight*, mix enough paint with water for the entire application. Apply it with a foam roller or foam brush.

tip

After you mix your paint, test it on a sample piece of similar fabric. Work quickly; textile paint dries fast, and the color lightens as it dries. Follow the heat setting instructions provided.

7. Once your surface is painted, let the fabric dry completely and then heat set the paint. Let your fabric air dry or use a blow dryer. Do not remove the painted fabric from your worktable until it is completely dry, or the paint will run. To heat set your fabric, set your iron on high and press with **no steam. Heat set your painted fabric from the back first,** ironing for at least five minutes to ensure the paint is set. Turn the fabric over and press for another five minutes.

tip

Use a pressing cloth when heat setting to prevent scorching.

Painting Details

Adding subtle details with textile paint can enhance your design. In *Fall* (page 74) my objective was to make the fence look distressed and old. I used watered-down textile paint along the top edges and sides of the fence and posts to create this illusion. In *New Zealand Adventure* (page 75) I used pearl-white textile paint to create the foam on the waves breaking on the shore. In *Winter Wonderland* (page 68) I opted to use an opaque white textile paint for snow on the dark brown trees because the tree fabric was so dark. In *Here Chickee, Chickee, Chickee* (page 56) I went a different direction, using a watered-down mixture of dark green and black textile paints for shading on the door.

Steps for Painting Details with Textile Paint

1. Do a test first, using a piece of similar fabric. Mix your paint on a plastic plate to the desired consistency and practice your painting techniques on scraps. Work with small amounts of textile paint when painting details. A little bit of paint goes a long way.

2. Use a small to medium-size artist brush.

3. Paint the details after the elements in your quilt have been basted or stitched. If you paint before stitching into place, the elements can shift or the edges might turn up.

4. To get the correct perspective, pin your quilt top onto your working wall and then paint the details with textile paint. In most cases, the paint will not bleed through onto your wall surface because the paint lies on top of the fabric.

tip

If you are apprehensive about the paint bleeding through to your working wall, place a piece of scrap muslin under the surface where you will be painting.

5. Dry the fabric and heat set the paint. **Be sure to use a pressing cloth** when pressing the front of your stabilized quilt top. The pressing cloth protects the invisible thread, netting, tulle, or organza from melting and also prevents scorching. After your painted fabric is heat set, it should not run or bleed.

6. Depending on the desired effect, you can incorporate two colors in tandem while you paint. Mix small amounts of paint next to one another on a plastic plate and dip your brush into both areas before applying the paint.

tip

As soon as you are finished painting, **immediately** wash your brushes or rollers with liquid detergent. Brushes will last for a very long time if you take good care of them.

Blending Colors

It is possible to create specific paint colors by mixing together more than one color of textile paint. There are some wonderful books on the market that explore textile painting in detail, including Mickey Lawler's *SkyDyes* and Vicki Johnson's *Paint and Patches* (see Bibliography).

Sponging

Using a sponge to create specific effects is a wonderful way to apply textile paint. Sponging is terrific for areas where you want the feeling of texture, such as rocks in the foreground, waves in the ocean, or snow on mountain peaks. The holes, dips, and crannies in the sponge allow you to see some of the background fabric through the paint, which adds realism. Natural sea sponges are best because the holes are not uniform, creating a more natural effect.

1. Unless you are sponging large areas of fabric, cut off a portion of the sea sponge, then cut this into several manageable pieces.

Sea sponge cut into small and manageable pieces for sponging

2. In most cases, use full-strength textile paint without water.

3. Wear gloves and place a small amount of paint on a plastic plate. Dip the sponge into the paint.

4. Blot the sponge one time on a doubled paper towel and then sponge directly onto a test fabric.

5. Once you are comfortable with your sponging test, sponge directly onto the surface of the quilt using light, quick movements. You can always add more paint but once you over-sponge it is too late!

Don't bother to save small pieces of used sea sponge because once the sponges are filled with paint, they are impossible to wash. When sponging larger areas on the surface of your quilt, use a large, uncut sea sponge. The large sponges can be saved. Wash with liquid detergent after each use.

6. Dry the fabric and heat set the paint as before.

Use a padded surface for stamping.

1. Place a piece of practice fabric on your padded stamping surface.

2. Dilute the textile paint so it is easy to spread but not runny.

3. Dip an artist or foam brush into the paint and spread a thin coat onto the stamp.

tip

Depending on the paint consistency, you might need to blot the stamp on a doubled paper towel before stamping.

4. Press the stamp down firmly onto the practice fabric, without twisting.

5. Lift the stamp straight up.

6. Make adjustments if necessary and then stamp directly onto your fabric.

7. Dry the fabric and heat set the paint using the same methods given earlier in this chapter.

tip

As you dip the sponge into the paint, change the position of the sponge often so you get different effects.

Stamping

Depending on the effect you want, it is possible to incorporate stenciling or stamping into your design. For example, in *Morning Glories Climbing Over the Gate* (page 60) I used a commercial leaf stamp and diluted textile paint for the leaves above the fence. Test the stamp using diluted textile paint on a piece of similar fabric until you find the right consistency for the paint. After blotting the stamp on a doubled paper towel several times, stamp directly onto the fabric, using a padded surface underneath. To achieve the desired effect of overlapping leaves and depth, stamp the closest leaves first and then stamp those leaves furthest in the distance last, **without applying more paint.**

tip

To make a padded surface for stamping, cover a piece of sturdy cardboard or heavy poster board with several layers of batting, approximately three inches thick. Cover the cardboard and batting with a piece of clear vinyl shelf paper or thick plastic, stretching it around to the back. Secure to the back with tape or staples.

tip

In addition to textile paint, commercial fabric stamp pads and fabric markers can be used for stamping.

Fabric Dye Pens and Artist Pencils

There are many occasions when you can use fabric dye pens or artist pencils to enhance landscape quilts. When you find a wonderful fabric but the value or color is wrong, change it yourself! If you are using a commercial grass fabric and the value of the grass is incorrect, you can change the color of the fabric with dye pens or artist pencils. The same holds true for flowers or any other element in nature. Using more than one color marker, or directional changes, adds realism and shading. Study the gate in *Morning Glories Climbing Over the Gate* (page 60). Some of the shading on the gate was accomplished with fabric markers.

1. Use any fabric dye pen or marker that can be heat set (see Resources).

tip

Always test fabric markers and pens or pencils before using them in your quilts. Take a piece of similar fabric and color it with markers or artist pencils. Heat set with an iron, **no steam**, back and front. Dip a white cloth into water and squeeze out most of the water. Rub the cloth over the colored portion. If the colored portion of the fabric runs or bleeds, shop for new markers!

2. Suppose you find the perfect fabric, except you want red roses instead of pink roses. No problem! Simply color the roses with a red marker and heat set. If you want your roses to have shading, press harder for darker areas and lighter in other areas. Think about using two shades of red instead of one. Your image will have dimension and will not appear flat.

3. There are times when using textile paint and markers or pencils that you might want a "smudged" appearance. In those cases, *do not* heat set your markers or pencils until after you smudge. For example, the fabric used for the chair in *Sanctuary* (page 61) was too stark and unrealistic. I colored the fabric with fabric markers, then smeared and smudged with a damp cloth until I got the desired effect. After the smudging I let the fabric dry, and then heat set it. I added detail lines around the edges in black to highlight the elements in the chair, then let the fabric dry and then heat set it again.

Fabric Bleaching

If you find a wonderful commercial print but the value is too dark, buy it anyway. Although the outcome is not always consistent, you can often bleach commercial fabrics to achieve a lighter value by following the steps for bleaching.

1. Wear a dust mask and gloves.

2. **Test a scrap of fabric first!**

3. Mix a 50/50 solution of water and bleach in a container large enough to accommodate the fabric.

4. Work next to a sink where you can rinse the fabric.

5. Immerse the fabric in the bleach solution.

6. Each commercial fabric is different. Some fabrics require immersion for a minute or two, while other fabrics may need to stay in the solution for five minutes or longer. Pay attention to how long you let it set, in order to reach the same results with your quilt fabric.

tip

Don't walk away—bleaching can be instantaneous. If the fabric sits in the solution too long, you risk over-bleaching and may end up with "holey" fabric.

7. When the desired value is reached, rinse immediately and wash with Synthrapol (available at most quilt shops), which will stop the bleaching action.

8. If you are pleased with the results of the test strip, you can now bleach the balance of the fabric with confidence.

Computer Magic

There will be times when you are unable to find commercial fabrics with the design elements you want to include in your quilt. Perhaps you want a birdbath or a garden chair in your next quilt and you just can't find a suitable fabric. If you are like me, drawing a birdbath or chair to scale is next to impossible. Why not use your computer to create what you need? When I created *Sanctuary* (page 61) I pictured an Adirondack chair under the tree. Since my original image did not have a chair, I created one.

Many people have a copyright-free greeting card program installed on their computer.

1. Locate the image you would like to use in your quilt.

2. Enlarge or reduce the size of the image on the page, if necessary.

3. Once the image is the correct size, print it out, then trace it onto your fabric and cut it out.

tip

If your program doesn't have an enlarging/reducing feature, simply print the image and use a color copy machine to enlarge or reduce it to the desired size.

Use computer magic to create details such as this chair in *Sanctuary* (page 61).

Printing Images Onto Computer Fabric

Another choice when using images from your computer is to print the image in color directly onto fabric that runs through your ink-jet or laser printer. There are two options for printing on fabric. Create the fabric yourself or purchase colorfast printer fabric at a quilt shop.

Creating Your Own Computer Fabric

1. Purchase a bottle of Bubble Jet solution from your local quilt shop.

2. Follow the manufacturer's instructions for preparing the fabric.

3. Add a backing to your fabric by ironing the shiny side of freezer paper to the wrong side of the fabric. This will help to avoid getting the fabric stuck in your printer.

4. Cut backed fabric to 8½" x 11".

Cotton sateen fabric, which has a wonderful sheen, is a better choice than bleached muslin. After your fabric is printed, rinse and dry according to the manufacturer's instructions, testing the fabric to make sure it does not run or bleed.

Prepared Fabric Printer Sheets

When I am in a pinch, I purchase fabric already prepared for a printer (see Resources). Follow the manufacturer's instructions for rinsing and heat setting, and test to make sure your image does not smear or bleed after it is heat set. I use the colorfast fabric sheets when making labels for my quilts. Label options are discussed in Chapter Twelve.

Printing the Color Image Onto Your Prepared Fabric

I'm including some basic instructions for using clip-art greeting card programs on PCs to print onto fabric. Each greeting card program is a little different, so follow the instructions in your particular program.

1. Open the clip-art program and select "New."

2. Select "Stationery" as the type of greeting card and select "Blank."

3. Select an 8" x 11" layout and hit "Insert graphic."

4. Search for your chosen image. When you find it, select "OK" to choose it. Adjust the size if necessary.

5. Select "Print", and go to "Setup."

6. Print a test copy on regular copy paper.

7. Cut out the test image, and audition it on your design.

8. Make any size adjustments and select "Setup" again. Hit "Options," select "Paper Type," choose "Greeting Card or Specialty Paper," and print on prepared fabric sheet.

tip

It may be necessary to manually guide freezer-paper-backed or prepared fabric sheets through the printer. When the rollers in the printer start to feed the fabric through, give it a little nudge to help it along.

Threadwork acts as an important embellishment in landscape quilts, adding dimension, depth, and texture. If you use thread in the wrong value or color, it can be distracting. I use many types of thread, and focus on the color rather than the manufacturer. I recommend a large variety of decorative threads: cotton machine embroidery, rayon, and variegated threads. I typically use 30, 40, and 12 weight threads, depending on my need.

tip

When purchasing thread, remember this tip: the smaller the number, the thicker the thread.

Twisted thread works well in landscape quilts because two complementary colors are twisted together into one thread, adding texture. I seldom use shiny threads because they don't seem realistic. There are times, however, when I deviate from this rule. Metallic and sliver threads are perfect for water, icy scenes, or the sun's reflection. Cotton 12 and 30 weight threads are wonderful for machine embroidery and easily go through the needle.

Adding Realism With Machine Embroidery

Why should I add machine embroidery to my design? It looks fine the way it is. Machine embroidery is an effective tool to enhance your quilt and give it depth and texture. Many quilters take specialized classes for machine embroidery techniques. I recommend you give yourself permission to play, and experiment with machine embroidery techniques *before* investing in a class. If you decide not to add threadwork to your landscape quilt, skip this step and proceed to Chapter Twelve for finishing techniques.

SETTING UP YOUR MACHINE

For machine embroidery I always do free-motion stitching. This means the feed dogs are dropped, a darning foot is attached, and the needle-down position is selected—if one is available on your sewing machine.

tip

I strongly recommend that any machine embroidery be completed *before* your quilt top is sandwiched with the batting and backing. It is easier to stitch extensively through one stabilized layer instead of three layers. Besides, you don't have to worry about how the back of your quilt top looks. You're the only one who will see it!

Hoopless in Seattle

Some quilters use a small wooden or plastic hoop, finger cots, or special gripping gloves when doing machine embroidery. I choose not to because I control the tension of my fabric with my hands while stitching.

1. In most cases, the amount of machine embroidery on your quilt top will be spread evenly across the surface.

Why spend so much time repositioning a hoop when you can accomplish the same goal using your hands?

2. How do you get the proper tension and ensure your quilt top doesn't pucker? Regardless of the size of your quilt, it is possible to roll the edges of your quilt top toward the center of your sewing machine, then grip those edges to manipulate and control the tension while doing machine embroidery. Maintain enough tension with your hands so the quilt has no puckers while you stitch.

tip

If you have a small quilt top, it is not necessary to roll the edges. Grip the outside edges of the top with enough tension so there is no puckering, but don't pull the quilt out of shape.

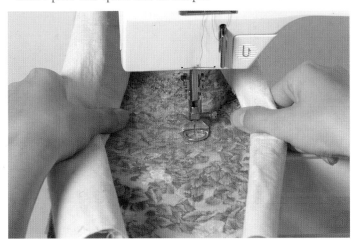

Control the sewing tension with your hands.

How and Where to Stitch

Changing thread can be the most frustrating part of machine embroidery. Unlike machine quilting, you can start your machine embroidery anywhere you want on your design. To save yourself time, energy, and frustration, instead of rethreading your machine each time you come to a section with a new color, jump to another section that can be stitched with the same color thread.

Machine embroider one color at a time.

1. Thread selection. Thread the top of your machine with a thread that matches your project. Use lightweight bobbin thread in your bobbin and a 75/11 machine embroidery needle.

2. Adjust the top and bobbin tensions. With practice, you'll be able to determine if the top tension on your machine is correct when you pull the thread through the needle. If the thread pulls through the needle too quickly, tighten your tension. Each machine is different and I cannot make specific recommendations regarding tension settings. The top tension on my sewing machine is typically set at two, one, or even zero when using specialty threads. Keep in mind the tension mechanism does not engage until you put your presser foot down. Don't forget to "walk" your bobbin to determine if the bobbin tension is correct. Refer to Chapter Four.

3. Practicing. Now it's time to practice. Using a stabilized piece of similar fabric, place your fabric under the presser foot. Pull the bobbin thread to the surface. With your machine in the needle-down position, take a few stitches in place to lock the threads, then trim them. Don't worry about how your embroidery looks on the back of the quilt. No one will see this stitching because it will be covered up when you sandwich your quilt.

Example of machine embroidery on the back of a quilt top

4. In which direction do I stitch? Machine embroidery should enhance your design and in almost all cases the stitches go in the same direction as the element portrayed. For example, if you begin stitching on a commercial grass print that basically goes up and down vertically, with an occasional crossover blade or two, then your stitching should follow the pattern as printed. If you are stitching water, the stitching direction should impart the

feeling or movement of the water. My experience is to duplicate what I see in nature when I machine embroider.

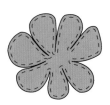

Embroider by following the shape of an element.

Enhance and expand the design element with machine embroidery.

5. Continue practicing on your sample fabric until you are happy with your stitches.

6. Sometimes is it is possible to add your own foliage, flowers, bushes, and so on using thread. Other times, it's better to accentuate what's already there. In *Here Chickee, Chickee, Chickee* (page 56) I used both of these techniques. The tall grasses and weeds growing up the wall were created with thread, while the remaining embroidery followed the pattern of individually cut shapes.

7. At times it will be easier to mimic elements using machine embroidery. Using this technique, it is not necessary to start, stop, and trim threads. In *English Garden* (page 41) I created small blue flowers between the preprinted blue clumps, allowing me to travel across the surface of the quilt without stopping. I mimicked the appearance of flowers by rotating the fabric in circles while stitching. A variegated blue thread accomplished several values within the clumps, doing much of the work for me.

tip

Use a bamboo skewer as you stitch to hold down any pesky edges.

Thread With an Attitude

Let's face it, thread is fickle. Like people, each particular thread has its own personality and doesn't always behave the way we want it to. Even though I have done extensive machine embroidery for many years, I still suffer thread nightmares from time to time and so will you. The following is my six-step method for eliminating thread nightmares.

1. With the presser foot down, adjust the top tension on your machine, changing the setting by two numbers.

2. Sometimes a thin coat of a silicone agent for thread solves a thread nightmare. If that doesn't fix the problem, go to Step 3.

3. Adjust the bobbin tension a quarter turn to the left. If that doesn't help, adjust the tension a quarter to half turn to the right.

4. If the thread is still balling up, breaking, or skipping, change your needle. Many times, this simple fix is the solution to your thread nightmare. If you are using a machine embroidery needle, try a Metallic needle. If that doesn't work, move on to a Topstitch or Jeans needle. You might need to adjust your top and bobbin thread tensions again when you change needles.

5. If you are still having problems, clean your sewing machine following the manufacturer's instructions, or have it professionally cleaned.

tip

When you reload your bobbin thread, clean your machine, the bobbin casing, and change your needle. Remove the presser cover, and take out the bobbin and the mechanism that holds the bobbin in place. Using a long-handled artist paintbrush, gently remove all dust, lint, and threads. Remove any threads that are stuck in the mechanism.

6. Try threading your bobbin thread through the little eye that is located on the arm portion of your bobbin casing. This will often solve your "threadache."

Thread the bobbin thread through the eye in the bobbin case arm.

7. If all else fails, try a different thread. Even substituting invisible thread in your bobbin can often do the trick. If that doesn't work, take two aspirins or have a glass of wine.

BOBBIN EMBROIDERY

There are times when you might want to use a thicker thread for machine embroidery that will not go through your needle. In my quilt *Fall* (page 74) I found a fluffy thread that I wanted to use for the pampas grass, but it was too thick to go through the needle. My quick and easy "road map method" provides a solution to this problem.

An example of machine embroidery from *Fall* using a thick thread in the bobbin

Making a Road Map

When you want to use a specific thread that will not go through the needle, simply make yourself a road map on the quilt top.

1. With invisible thread in the top, and black thread in the bobbin, stitch around the areas you want to define on the top of the quilt.

2. The thread on the top of the quilt is invisible and the black thread or road map is on the back of the quilt.

3. Fill your bobbin with the thick thread and place it in your bobbin casing. You will need to adjust the bobbin tension to accommodate the thicker thread. Keep the invisible thread in the top of your machine and adjust the tension as necessary. Turn your quilt top over, and with the back facing up, stitch following your road map, filling in as necessary.

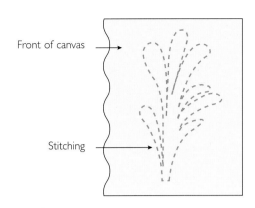

Use invisible thread on top and black bobbin thread to outline an element to be embroidered.

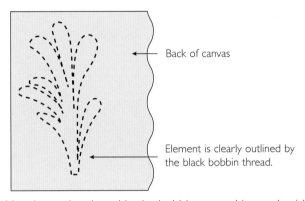

Use decorative thread in the bobbin to machine embroider the outlined area with the back facing up.

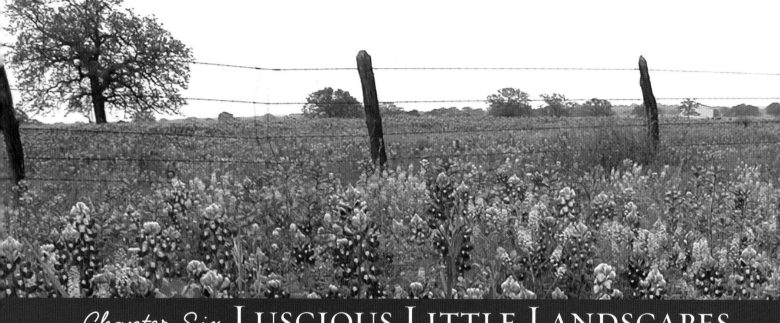

First Quilts

This chapter includes projects and examples suitable for all levels of quilters, especially beginners. Your first project should be a simple design without excess detail, giving you the opportunity to create and finish a project and feel proud of your efforts. Depending on your design, a good size for your first quilt is approximately 26" by 20". Don't start too small, as miniatures are more difficult. Making a large landscape quilt for your first project isn't advisable, as you should enjoy yourself without becoming overwhelmed. You certainly don't want your first landscape project to end up as just another UFO!

Using Preprinted Commercial Panels

Using commercial preprinted panels in landscape quilts is perfectly acceptable. In fact, I highly recommend incorporating commercial panels into your designs because it simplifies the process. To demonstrate how easy it is to incorporate preprinted panels into your design, study the quilts *English Garden*, *Sunset*, and *Blue Mountains* included in this chapter.

ENGLISH GARDEN

English Garden by Joyce R. Becker, 22" x 23", 2001

inspiration

When I saw the bolt of commercial fabric with repeating flowers and cottages, I fell in love with it. I knew this fabric would be perfect to include in kits for a workshop I teach, *Special Effects for Realistic Landscape Quilts*. My goal was to make a quilt that would be perfect for beginning landscape quilters to learn the basic steps of designing on the wall, cutting, gluing, placement, and stitching.

BASICS

English Garden uses four commercial fabrics and can be designed and stitched with invisible thread in six hours or less!

MATERIALS

- Stabilized muslin canvas: 20" x 21"
- Cottage/floral panel, multicolored, one repeat: ½ yard
- Coordinating floral preprinted, multicolored: ½ yard
- Rock print, same value and size, light brown: ½ yard
- Background sky, pale blue: ½ yard
- Tulle overlay (optional), white: ½ yard

- Border, backing, binding, and sleeve, dark magenta: 2 yards
- Batting: 25" x 28"
- Textile paint: Green, close in value to preprinted trees
- Artist paintbrush: Medium
- Fabric markers: Green, yellow, orange, and white

If you find a sky fabric that is just a little too strong, turn it over and use the back of the fabric.

Fabrics used in *English Garden*

CUTTING

Border: Cut four 4½" strips of dark magenta.

Binding: Cut three 2½" strips of dark magenta.

Sleeve: Cut one 8½" strip of dark magenta.

CONSTRUCTION

Design, Cut, Glue, and Baste

1. Follow the basic instructions for creating a canvas as described in Chapter One.

2. Prestarch all of the fabrics except for the sky.

3. Position and pin the sky fabric onto the top half of your canvas. Make sure your sky extends far enough into the design; the sky shows behind the trees, about halfway down the canvas. Baste the sky onto the canvas with invisible thread.

4. Cut the design features from the prestarched cottage panel. Start by cutting out the trees. Position and glue them into place over the sky fabric on the canvas. Continue to build your design from the top down. Make sure the trees are not all the same shape or height and that the edges of your shapes are rounded, with no blunt edges.

5. Place and glue the cottage beneath and in front of the trees.

6. Build the pathway once the cottage is in place. The rocks should be smaller in the distance and larger in the foreground, at the bottom of the design.

7. Incorporate the other floral print, leaving some areas of green or negative space in your design.

8. Cut, position, and glue the fence into place.

9. Continue to build on your design. Place flowers along the edge of the pathway, and along the fence.

Sample of design progression, *English Garden*

10. Review your design. Is it balanced? Are the trees different heights and shapes? Are the shapes natural? Is there enough open or negative space?

11. Baste the entire composition with invisible thread.

PAINTING AND MACHINE EMBROIDERY

1. This step is optional. Mix green textile paint with a small amount of water on a plastic plate. Add painted trees to the left side of your design, using the photograph of the quilt as a guide. Dry and heat set. To highlight the leaves and add dimension and fall colors, add small dots of color to the trees with fabric markers. Heat set.

2. Place an overlay of tulle over the painted trees. Baste with invisible thread and trim.

3. If desired, add machine embroidery techniques as described in Chapter Five.

4. Follow the Fine Finishing Techniques as described in Chapter Twelve to complete your quilt.

Sunset by Joyce R. Becker, 25" × 25", 1999

A preprinted fabric panel by Nancy Crow inspired *Sunset*. My goal was to "pump up" this scene, adding more texture and realism with additional trees and foliage and a wider variety of foreground fabrics. This quilt gave me the opportunity to play with distance and perspective through the use of overlays.

BASICS

The panel portion of this quilt includes only the sky and the first row of trees. The foreground includes several commercial fabrics in similar values depicting grass, rocks, and foliage. I incorporated a light source in this design, giving the feel of the setting sun coming in from the right side of the quilt. To accomplish this objective, I painted the upper-right portion of the sky with gold textile paint, placed a layer of gold tulle over the paint and stitched with metallic gold thread.

MATERIALS

- Stabilized muslin canvas: 22" x 22"
- Preprinted commercial panel in orange, gold, avocado green, brown: 1 panel approx. ½ yard
- Foliage in several commercial prints in orange, golden-brown, avocado green: ½ yard of each
- Foreground fabric, greenish brown: ½ yard
- Overlay, medium brown tulle: 1 yard
- Overlay gold tulle: ½ yard
- Inner border, medium brown: ⅜ yard
- Outer border, backing, binding, and sleeve, golden orange: 2 yards
- Batting: 28" x 28"
- Textile paint: Metallic gold
- Artist paintbrush: Medium

CUTTING

Inner border: Cut four 2" strips of brown.

Outer border: Cut four 3½" strips of golden orange.

Binding: Cut three 2½" strips of golden orange.

Sleeve: Cut one 8½" strip of golden orange.

CONSTRUCTION

Design, Cut, Glue, and Baste

1. Follow the basic instructions for creating a canvas as described in Chapter One.

2. Press the panel. Position it onto the canvas and pin it into place.

3. Cut, position, and pin the foreground fabric into place. Baste the panel and the foreground fabrics.

4. Use a matching avocado thread to machine embroider a second row of trees below the first row of trees.

5. Prestarch and fussy cut foliage fabrics. Position and glue into place.

6. Baste the entire composition with invisible thread.

MACHINE EMBROIDERY AND PAINTING

1. Add machine embroidery to the foliage, if desired.

2. Paint the upper right portion of the sky with gold textile paint. Dry and heat set.

3. Machine embroider the sky with a shiny gold metallic thread to simulate the sunset.

4. Place an overlay of gold tulle on the right side of the sky. Baste and trim.

5. Place an overlay of medium-brown tulle over the entire top to blend the colors together. Baste the tulle around the outside perimeter of the quilt.

6. Follow the Fine Finishing Techniques as described in Chapter Twelve to complete your quilt.

BLUE MOUNTAINS

inspiration

This quilt-in-progress demonstrates how simple it is to use two preprinted commercial panel fabrics to make a landscape quilt. In this case, I used a preprinted cloud fabric and a Nancy Crow panel with preprinted mountains and water. I include this quilt for teaching purposes to demonstrate how to incorporate panels into your work and how layering with tulle or using fabric markers can tone down values. I also show you how to enhance preprinted panels with other elements, such as rocks and trees, to make your design more realistic and to add visual interest.

Blue Mountains (in progress) by Joyce R. Becker

BASICS

Notice the subtle differences between the left- and right-hand sides of the quilt. I toned down the mountain and water values with dye pens to suggest a cloudy versus a bright moonlit sky. I then layered a single piece of dark blue tulle over the right side of the quilt to mute the value. Can you see the difference in the water? Using metallic thread, I stitched over the tulle to give the feeling of moving water. The rock fabric on the right side of the quilt was stitched with a variegated chartreuse thread to create moss. These subtle changes add more realism to your quilt.

MATERIALS

- Stabilized muslin canvas: 27" x 27"
- Mountain and water panel, dark blue: 1 panel approximatly 1 yard
- Cloud panel, dark blue hues: ½ yard
- Rocks, light to medium brown: ½ yard
- Tree bark, medium brown: ½ yard

- Overlay, dark blue tulle: ½ yard
- Backing, binding, and sleeve, dark blue: 1½ yards
- Batting: 27" x 27"
- Fabric markers: Several values of dark blue and purple
- Thread to match fabric

CUTTING

Binding: Cut three 2½" strips of dark blue.

Sleeve: Cut one 8½" strip of dark blue.

CONSTRUCTION

Design, Cut, Glue, and Baste

1. Follow the basic instructions for creating a canvas as described in Chapter One.

2. Press the cloud panel. Position, pin, and baste the cloud fabric to canvas.

3. Prestarch mountain/water panel. Cut, position, and glue the mountain/water panel into place.

4. Mute the reflections in the water by using darker values of blue and purple markers. Heat set.

5. Place a layer of dark blue tulle over the quilt top. Pin into place.

6. Cut, position, and glue the rock formations and the tree into place.

7. Baste the entire composition.

MACHINE EMBROIDERY AND PAINTING

1. Machine embroider the water using a variegated blue thread to suggest movement.

2. Add moss to the rocks with machine embroidery. Rotate fabric and stitch in small circles. Use a variegated chartreuse green thread.

3. Machine embroider the pine tree needles onto the trees, using a medium-dark green embroidery thread.

4. Follow the Fine Finishing Techniques as described in Chapter Twelve to complete your quilt.

PORT TOWNSEND AUTUMN

inspiration

Allie Aller made this luscious little landscape after attending a quilting conference in Port Townsend, Washington. She did not use a printed visual image for her inspiration, saying, "My quilt was a direct result of being in the landscape I portrayed." Allie worked on her design wall, collage style, using a foundation canvas as I do.

Port Townsend Autumn by Allison Aller, Washougal, Washington, 20" × 18", 1999, photograph courtesy of Bill Bachhuber

BASICS

Allie sandwiches her backing, batting, and foundation muslin together with spray adhesive before assembling her collage. When her collage or design is done, she stitches and quilts with invisible thread in one step. Allie feels her greatest accomplishment in this quilt is "conveying a real sense of depth or distance."

Detail, *Port Townsend Autumn*

tips

If you are at a quilting class or conference, don't be shy about collecting scraps from the floor at the end of the day! They can be useful in a small quilt.

You should walk away from your landscape for a few days before stitching it down. It often needs last minute tweaking; fresh eyes can see what changes, if any, are needed.

TWILIGHT AT PARADISE

inspiration

Twilight at Paradise by Joyce R. Becker, 24" x 28", 2002, inspired by a watercolor painting by William Winden

This quilt was inspired by a greeting card by acclaimed watercolor artist William Winden. A place of continual spiritual reinforcement, Mt. Rainier is one of the most beautiful places in the world. I am so fortunate to be able to witness this gorgeous mountain from my backyard deck when it is not shrouded in clouds. *Twilight at Paradise* pays homage to this magical area as the sun sets. Paradise, however, is a play on words. It is also the name of a quaint village located at the base of a popular hiking trail on Mt. Rainier.

BASICS

Easy enough for a beginner, the entire quilt, including basting, sandwiching, quilting, blocking, and binding, can be completed in two days. This piece is suitable for practicing machine embroidery. The rock formations on the mountain are a snap using my secret weapon: dryer lint. Once your mountain is in place on your canvas, shape and mold small bits of lint directly onto the mountain. Save medium to medium-dark dryer lint just for this purpose. After the formations are complete, cover the mountain with an overlay of white polyester organza and baste with invisible thread.

MATERIALS

- Stabilized muslin canvas: 30" x 34"
- Sky, medium to dark blue, several values: ½ yard
- Mountain, white cotton sateen or bleached white muslin: ½ yard
- Mountain overlay, white polyester organza: ½ yard
- Trees, dark green with several values (double the layers for bonding): ½ yard
- Trees, medium green with several values (double the layers for bonding): ½ yard
- Foliage, medium green portraying shrubs, several values: ¾ yard
- Grass, medium/dark green, several values, long blades: ½ yard
- Flowers, periwinkle/purple with increasing scale (extra for bonded flowers): 1 yard
- Flowers, yellow, small scale: ½ yard
- Binding, mottled dark blue: ⅜ yard
- Backing and sleeve, gray: 1 yard
- Batting: 27" x 31"
- Fusible web: 1½ yards
- Dryer lint, dark to medium gray-blue (Denim lint is perfect!)
- Optional: Shiny beads for twinkling stars
- Threads to match fabric
- #2 pencil

CUTTING

Binding: Cut three 2½" strips of mottled dark blue.

Sleeve: Cut one 8½" strip of gray.

CONSTRUCTION

Design, Cut, Glue, and Baste

1. Follow the basic instructions for creating a canvas as described in Chapter One.

2. Prestarch all the fabrics *except* sky and organza.

3. Position, pin, and glue the sky fabrics onto your canvas.

4. Draw a mountain on the cotton sateen or muslin. Cut just below the drawing line.

5. Position, pin, and baste the top edge of the mountain to the sky. **Do not** baste along the sides and bottom of the mountain. Trim the excess sky fabric behind the mountain so it will not create a shadow.

6. Cut the top edge of the background foliage fabric to depict bushes, shrubs, and trees of different heights. Position, glue, and baste the foliage into place.

7. Bond two similar layers of the dark green tree fabric, wrong sides together. Cut trees of different sizes.

8. Bond together two similar layers of the medium-green tree fabric, wrong sides together. Cut tree shapes of different sizes.

9. Audition, position, and glue the trees into place.

Positioning background foliage into place.

10. Cut clumps of periwinkle blue flowers. Start with the flowers in the smallest scale. Place these small flowers in the distance (nearer the top of your design). Work forward, placing the larger flowers closer to the foreground (the bottom of the design). Add definition by cutting around individual petals and position the flower on top of the background foliage. Increase the density of flowers as you work forward.

Cutting clumps of flowers

11. Follow the natural shape of the grass fabric as you cut clumps. Position and glue grass into place. Check the placement, and adjust if necessary.

Cutting grass fabrics

12. Baste the entire composition.

MACHINE EMBROIDERY AND PAINTING

1. If desired, add texture and dimension with machine embroidery. Optional: Add shiny beads in the sky.

2. Follow the Fine Finishing Techniques as described in Chapter Twelve to complete your quilt.

3. Add bonded three-dimensional flowers to "fall" off the bottom of the quilt after binding, at the bottom edge of the quilt. Glue into place and stitch through the centers of the flowers with invisible thread.

Shiny beads twinkle in the night sky.

Use dryer lint to add dimension and texture to the mountains.

Trees and shrubs are embroidered.

Flowers fall over the edge.

First Frost by Joyce R. Becker, 26" × 20", 2002

inspiration

My source of inspiration for this quilt was a sentiment rather than a photograph or visual image. I live in an area where the seasonal changes are often dramatic. When summer begins to fade into fall, the fields of fat, orange pumpkins ripen with the first frost. The air feels different, crisp and charged with energy. This quilt celebrates the first frost of autumn, pumpkins aplenty, leaves turning vivid colors, and bouquets of flowers showing off their final blossoms.

BASICS

A gorgeous chartreuse, hand-dyed fabric from Just Imagination (see Resources) was the background for this quilt. When shopping for a similar background, make sure there are several values and areas that suggest dappled light filtering through. This quilt requires little time and the machine embroidery is optional. If you are unable to find a preprinted basket and rake, enlarge and copy my images. Or use your computer clip-art programs, as I did, and print your own basket and rake onto computer fabric (see Chapter Four).

MATERIALS

Note: A muslin canvas is not necessary. Use your stabilized background fabric as your canvas.

- Background, backing, binding, and sleeve, chartreuse: 2 yards
- Tree leaves, small-scale leaves in gold, orange, red, bright rose, and green: 1 yard total
- Flower leaves: Chartreuse/yellow/dark green veins with appearance of dying leaves: 1 yard
- Flowers, bright rose/pink in correct scale resembling geraniums: 1 yard
- Pumpkins, preprinted orange pumpkins with vines, shrubs: ½ yard

- Apples/Basket, preprinted apple/basket: ½ yard
- Weathered flower box, dark brown woodgrained: ½ yard
- Shrubs, mottled chartreuse (double for bonding): ¾ yard
- Shrubs and vines: Medium green: ½ yard
- Tree branches, dark brown: ¼ yard
- Fusible web: 2 yards
- Batting: 29" x 23"
- Fabric markers: Several values of medium to dark brown
- Thread to match fabrics

Bond two layers of similar leaf fabric to make cutting easier.

CUTTING

Background: Cut a 32" x 26" rectangle of chartreuse.

Binding: Cut three 2½" strips of chartreuse.

Sleeve: Cut one 8½" strip of chartreuse.

CONSTRUCTION

Design, Cut, Glue, and Baste

1. Press background fabric to remove all creases or wrinkles. Stabilize the background with fusible interfacing. Place the stabilized background on your design wall.

2. Cut, position, and glue the tree limbs into place.

3. Fuse two layers of similar tree leaf fabric with wrong sides together. Cut out individual leaves. Position and glue leaves into place. Save extra leaves to position onto the grass in the foreground and on the leaf basket.

4. Enlarge and copy the flower box as pictured. Trace the flower box onto weathered woodgrain fabric. Cut, position, and glue into place.

5. Cut flowers and leaves from the prebonded fabrics and position so they flow over the edge of the weathered flower box. Tuck some of the flowers behind the leaves.

6. Enlarge and copy the leaf basket and rake as pictured. Or create your own images using a computer clip-art program and computer fabric (see Chapter Four). Cut, position, and glue into place. Position extra leaves around the base of the leaf basket.

7. Cut, position, and glue the pumpkins, apples, and the small basket into place.

8. Cut foliage and vines. Position and glue into place.

9. Cut large foliage stalks from bonded chartreuse fabric (pictured in front of flower box). Position and glue into place.

10. Baste the composition with invisible thread.

MACHINE EMBROIDERY AND PAINTING

1. Use the matching and medium-green variegated threads to add machine embroidery highlights to the grassy area in the foreground on the left side. Use the same medium-green thread to enhance foliage, stalks, and vines by following the natural shape of the element.

2. Add dimension to the flowers with machine embroidery by using a medium-rose embroidery thread. Follow the natural shape of each flower.

3. Add twigs to the tree branches and veins to the flowers with a matching dark brown thread. This step can be done before or after the leaves are positioned and basted into place.

4. Shade the leaf basket with fabric markers, and heat set.

5. Follow the Fine Finishing Techniques as described in Chapter Twelve to complete your quilt.

Winter Visitor

Winter Visitor by Rosellen Carolan, Kent, Washington, 26" × 28", 1999

By using the scenic, snowy-mountain fabric and surrounding it with fabric representing deciduous woods in the winter, Rosy said, "I was able to combine memories of the Oklahoma woods of my childhood and the Cascade Mountains of Washington I enjoy as an adult. I immediately thought of a winter landscape that included a red cardinal, one of my favorite winter birds from childhood. Once I decided on the cardinal, I needed a tree for it to perch on, so I chose a simple, couched yarn tree. It took quilting to help me realize there is a creative soul in each of us, waiting to be released." Specifically designed for a guild challenge using only black and white fabrics and no more than five inches of red, this charming landscape was a prize-winning entry.

Basics

Rosy creates her landscape quilts in a fashion similar to mine, designing on a canvas on the wall. Reflecting on her quilt, Rosy said, "Finding just the right combination of fabrics in the correct scale was crucial to the visual impact of the piece." Working with just four fabrics, she pieced frames around the off-center scenic mountain fabric, gluing and couching the tree with a zigzag stitch using invisible thread.

tip

Use a few small dots of water-soluble basting glue to hold the yarn in place during the couching process. The yarn stays exactly where you put it.

RED SKIES AT NIGHT, SAILOR'S DELIGHT

inspiration

Living in the Pacific Northwest, I am constantly in awe of the beauty around me. From the stunning mountains to the rough and tumble coastlines, I am inspired to translate these magnificent vistas into landscape quilts. *Red Skies at Night, Sailors Delight* was inspired by the myriad of lighthouses along the rugged coastlines of Oregon and Washington. I worked from a mental image of what I wanted to portray rather than from one specific photo.

Red Skies at Night, Sailor's Delight by Joyce R. Becker, 48" × 47", 2000, photograph courtesy of Mark Frey

BASICS

Initially I wanted to create a scene with a colorful sky using a wonderful array of hand-dyed fabric. Creating a cohesive sky wasn't as simple as anticipated. Extensive machine embroidery with coordinating thread helped to blend the colors together. Finding the right water fabric was difficult, so I painted the water with textile paint on cotton sateen fabric (see Resources). I strategically placed the rocks from a commercial print in formations mimicking what I see in nature, with the larger boulders nearest to the foreground.

MATERIALS

- Stabilized muslin canvas: 43" x 42"
- Water, white cotton sateen: 2 yards
- Rocks, brown commercial rock print: 1 yard
- Sky, blue, magenta, yellow, red: 2 yards
- Foliage, medium green/yellow: ½ yard
- Lighthouse, off-white crackled plaster print: ½ yard
- Lighthouse beacon, bright yellow/gold: ¼ yard
- Beacon overlay, white polyester organza: ¼ yard
- Lighthouse cording, black, ¼" width: 1 yard
- Lighthouse roof, red: ¼ yard
- Lighthouse windows, black: ¼ yard
- Inner border, magenta: 1 yard
- Outer border, backing, sleeve and binding, blue: 4 yards
- Batting: 51" x 50"
- Paint: Blue opaque and white pearl
- Fabric markers: Brown and gray
- Artist paintbrush: Medium
- Freezer paper

CUTTING

Inner border: Cut five 2" strips of magenta.

Outer border: Cut six 4½" strips of blue.

Binding: Cut five 2½" strips of blue.

Sleeve: Cut two 8½" strips of blue.

CONSTRUCTION

Design, Cut, Glue, and Baste

1. Follow the basic instructions for creating a canvas as described in Chapter One.

2. Prestarch all fabrics except the water and overlays.

3. Cut elliptical shapes out of sky fabrics and glue into place, using a transitional fabric to blend the colors together.

Use elliptical shapes for the different areas of the sky.

tip

A transitional fabric picks up the color families of the areas you are trying to blend.

4. Cut white cotton sateen to desired size for water. Paint with blue opaque textile paint as described in Chapter Four. Dry and heat set.

5. Pin the water onto the canvas. Baste the water to the sky using invisible thread; also baste around the outside perimeter.

6. Draw, trace, or copy a lighthouse, enlarging or reducing the design as necessary to fit. Transfer the design onto shiny side of freezer paper. Iron the shiny side of the freezer paper onto the wrong side of the lighthouse fabric.

7. Add a ¼" seam allowance and cut out the design. Turn under a ¼" seam allowance, and press.

8. Remove the freezer paper, position the lighthouse onto the canvas, and glue into place.

9. Cut out a circle of gold/yellow fabric for the beacon. Position and glue it into place, referring to the photograph. Cover the beacon with organza.

10. Place and glue black cording for the railing. Refer to the photograph for placement.

11. Draw and cut the window shapes from the black fabric, using the photograph as a guide.

12. Trace and cut the lighthouse roof from red fabric. Glue it into place.

13. Cut the commercial rock fabric into natural-looking groupings. Place the smaller rocks in the distance, and the larger rocks closer to the foreground. Refer to cutting instructions in Chapter Three.

14. Cut the foliage fabric and glue it into place along the shore.

15. Baste the entire composition with invisible thread. Refer to Chapter Four for basting instructions.

MACHINE EMBROIDERY AND PAINTING

1. Place your quilt top on your working wall. Use pearl-white textile paint to paint foam and waves in the water. Refer to Chapter Four for basic heat setting instructions.

When painting, start with the area that is closest to the top and work down.

2. Use machine embroidery to marry the layers of the sky into a cohesive unit by using a thread that blends together the color families.

3. Use the photograph as a guide to add detail and shading to the rocks with fabric markers. Heat set.

4. Satinstitch the outline of the lighthouse using matching or invisible thread.

5. Use black thread to satinstitch around the windows on the lighthouse.

6. Couch the cording with a zigzag stitch using black thread.

To couch: Stitch over the top of the black cording using a zigzag stitch and black thread.

7. Add texture and detail to the foliage with machine embroidery using a variegated green and yellow thread.

8. Add texture to the rocks, using a variety of brown and gray threads. Use the darkest value thread near the water line.

Detail of *Red Skies at Night, Sailor's Delight*

9. Machine embroider the water using a light to dark blue variegated thread. Be sure the stitching is horizontal.

10. Follow the Fine Finishing Techniques as described in Chapter Twelve to complete your quilt.

Stitching example for water

KAIKOURA ROCKS
inspiration

Kaikoura Rocks by Marie Blennerhassett, New Plymouth, New Zealand, 20" × 26", 2001, photograph courtesy of Roger French

A star pupil and prize-winning appliqué artist, Marie quickly grasped my methodology during a workshop I taught at the Quilting Symposium in New Zealand. I'm not sure who was more excited during the creation of her stunning quilt, Marie or I. Armed with a cache of perfect fabrics, Marie had her design on the wall in no time. She said, "I enjoy everything about the quilt, especially the way the rocks turned out." A photograph Marie saw in the newspaper featuring the New Zealand Stamp Collection was the inspiration for her quilt.

BASICS

With a bit of encouragement, Marie added the realistic shading/texture on the rocks with sponging and fabric markers.

tip

Don't be afraid to add shadows and shading with fabric markers. Using markers for shading on the rocks really paid off in Marie's quilt.

WILD AND FREE
inspiration

This playful and colorful underwater landscape quilt was inspired by a calendar. Saying she was "a little overwhelmed at first, not knowing quite how to start," Carol jumped right in anyway, and began cutting and gluing fabric. As she placed and rearranged the pieces, Carol said the lightbulb finally went on, and "voila!" the quilt just fell into place.

Giving herself permission to play, Carol transformed a plain, ordinary fish into a shimmering, colorful, and realistic portrayal using iridescent threads and fabric.

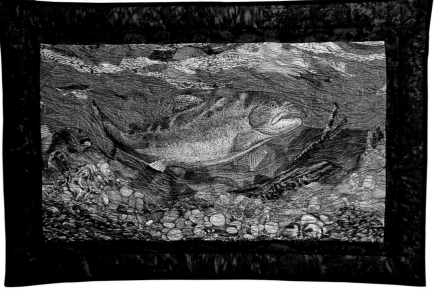

Wild and Free by Carol Smith Mackenzie, Wasco, Oregon, 40" × 26", 2000, photograph courtesy of Jeff King

tip

Use a double needle and shiny threads to give waves movement and a sense of motion.

HERE CHICKEE, CHICKEE, CHICKEE

inspiration

Sometimes inspiration comes directly from the fabric. Two dramatic hand-painted SkyDye (see Resources) fabrics compelled me to create this nostalgic garden scene. When I spotted the chicken fabric, I knew I *had* to make a garden quilt—or three—that included chickens. A secret garden door suggests mystery. When my dear friend Patti Cunningham saw *Here Chickee, Chickee, Chickee,* she exclaimed, "I must have this quilt!" My husband even pleaded her case, saying, "Surely you can find the time to make such a good friend a quilt." Thus, *Patti's Chickens* (page 81) was born. With a deadline looming for another quilt, I figured "what the heck," and made one more chicken quilt. Designed specifically for the Association of Pacific Northwest Quilters *Telling Secrets* Traveling Exhibit and Auction, *Chickens Guarding My Secret Garden* (page 82), will be auctioned at the 2004 Pacific Northwest QuiltFest in Seattle, Washington.

Here Chickee, Chickee, Chickee by Joyce R. Becker, 23" × 27", 2001

BASICS

This quilt is a breeze to make if you have the right fabrics. A suggestion: Save yourself some time and buy the garden wall and door fabrics. Referring to the photograph of the quilt, shop for vine-like leaf fabrics that are the correct scale and value. To make cutting easier, bond together two layers of similar leaf fabric. Shop for a variety of foliage prints in different values to add visual interest to your quilt as described in Chapter Two. You can paint a brown chicken with white opaque textile paint, or vice versa. Highlight the chicken with machine embroidery using white thread. Accomplish the shading on the door with watered-down textile paints and fabric markers.

MATERIALS

- Stabilized muslin canvas: 22" x 26"
- Background fabric, dark green mottled print (between brick wall and door): ¼ yard
- Brick wall, gray: ¾ yard
- Door, medium brown/gold: ½ yard
- Vines, medium green, correct scale and good definition (doubled for bonding): 1½ yards
- Flowers, small scale, red: ¼ yard
- Foreground, medium green to chartreuse: ½ yard
- Foliage, a variety of prints, medium to dark green: ¼ yard cuts
- Chicken print: ½ yard
- Inner border, mottled red: ½ yard
- Outer border, backing, binding, and sleeve, gray batik: 2 yards
- Batting: 26" x 31"
- Fabric markers: Dark and medium brown and rust for door
- Paint: Black and dark green, for shading on door, white opaque for chicken
- Threads to match fabric
- Artist paintbrush: medium

CUTTING

Between the door and the wall: Cut one 6" strip of dark green mottled print.

Inner border: Cut four 1½" strips of red.

Outer border: Cut four 3" strips of gray batik.

Binding: Cut three 2½" strips of gray batik.

Sleeve: Cut one 8½" strip of gray batik.

CONSTRUCTION

Design, Cut, Glue, and Baste

1. Follow the basic instructions for creating a canvas as described in Chapter One.

2. Prestarch all of the fabrics.

3. Position and glue the dark green fabric into place behind the door.

4. Cut, position, and glue foreground chartreuse fabric into place.

5. Cut out a door background, referring to the photograph of the quilt. Cut additional door parts, and glue them onto the door. Position and glue the entire door into place.

6. Cut, position, and glue gray brick walls into place to the left of the door and to the right of the green fabric behind the door.

Cut the wall so it is imperfect and not straight up and down; it should look weathered or distressed.

7. Cut, position, and glue individual leaf and flower shapes into place. Tuck some of the flowers underneath the leaves so they "peek out." Refrain from adding too many flowers.

8. Paint one brown chicken white. Dry and heat set. Cut chickens from fabric, position, and glue into place.

9. Fussy cut foliage from fabric. Position and glue into place, in front of the wall.

tip

If desired, bond two layers of one or two of the foliage prints so some of the foliage is three-dimensional (see Chapter Three). Consider adding some bonded foliage after the borders are added, so the foliage "falls" over the edge.

10. Baste entire composition with invisible thread.

MACHINE EMBROIDERY AND PAINTING

1. Add shading on the door with fabric markers and diluted textile paint. Dry and heat set.

2. Machine embroider vines that twist through leaves on the brick walls.

3. Machine embroider other elements with matching thread.

4. Follow the Fine Finishing Techniques as described in Chapter Twelve to complete your quilt.

Detail of *Here Chickee, Chickee, Chickee*

JERUSALEM
inspiration

Natalie said "this quilt came into being seemingly on its own" without extensive revisions and additions. Her truly remarkable quilt was inspired by a visit with her sister who lives in a small town on the outskirts of Jerusalem. Arriving in March, Natalie found the meadows in full bloom. To her, "the contrast between the ancient olive trees and the new abundant poppies seemed to symbolize the ancient city itself, with all its new outgrowth." An award-winning landscape quilt artist, Natalie's work has been featured on the television series *Sewing with Nancy*. Natalie co-authored *Landscape Quilts* with Nancy Zieman (see Bibliography).

Jerusalem by Natalie Sewell, Madison, Wisconsin, 68" × 55", 2002, photograph courtesy of Dale Hall Photography

BASICS

Natalie's goal was to "capture the sense of antiquity in the olive tree," conveying its age and texture. She used eight fabrics in her tree trunk, along with fabric paint, to intensify the light and shadows. Wanting to experience her techniques first-hand, I sat in on a workshop Natalie taught. We exchanged ideas, processes, and thoughts in an open-minded atmosphere of sharing, and an endearing friendship blossomed as a result.

tip

Natalie says one of the hardest things she had to do was teach herself to "cut badly. My foreground and distant shrubbery always looked stilted until I learned to shred fabric and zigzag the scissors as I cut."

MORNING GLORIES CLIMBING OVER THE GATE

inspiration

This quilt was created in a workshop with Natalie Sewell. Recalling a painting I saw of an old gate in a how-to book, I decided to create my own garden scene, including a weather-beaten gate as the focal point. I planned my design prior to class, stamping the leaves above the gate with diluted textile paint. Since morning glories are a favorite flower of mine, I decided to "plant" them in my scene on vines twisting, turning, twining, and climbing over the weathered old gate. This quilt always makes me smile. Filled with wonder and curiosity, the flowers peek through the vines at the break of day, anxious to greet the sun.

Morning Glories Climbing Over the Gate by Joyce R. Becker, 27" × 35", 2000

BASICS

Thinking through my process in advance was key. Wanting my scene to look like a watercolor painting, I stenciled leaves on the background sky fabric. I used a large variety of leaf prints in different values but similar size. Some of the leaves and flowers are fused and three-dimensional. The flowers and leaves in the distance were cut smaller, and an overlay of white tulle helps them appear further away. Flowers were highlighted with fabric markers and machine embroidery to deepen their hues. The foreground fabric was darkened with a fabric marker to make it look more realistic (lighter in the distance, darker in the foreground).

Sanctuary by Joyce R. Becker, 28" × 31", 1999

inspiration

When I studied art history in college, I became enamored with the impressionistic works of the artist Claude Monet. Wanting to create a quilt with an impressionistic feel that would also incorporate the mood of Thomas Kinkade, I set out to create an original design paying homage to both artists. My design changed dramatically as it progressed; my original vision was replaced by a totally different translation.

BASICS

In this quilt, the true inspiration was a rubber stamp of a gazebo. After stamping the gazebo on a piece of fabric, cutting it, and positioning it on my background fabric, I began building my garden scene with no preplanning. Modestly speaking, this quilt turned into quite a learning process. My original design had water and preprinted trees that seemed to float unrealistically into the heavens. The pastel palette of colors I selected for my original garden seemed lifeless and flat. I replaced the displeasing elements with colorful substitutions. Reworking this quilt taught me so much. I learned to take risks, realizing it is perfectly acceptable to change and modify quilts during their progression.

tip

When creating a design with a path or walkway, form the pathway before positioning the flowers and foliage.

MIDWINTER TROPICAL DREAMSCAPE

inspiration

Jane Moxey is a writer and producer for a popular PBS television special featuring quilts of the Pacific Northwest QuiltFest. She likes the "timeless, placeless, dream-like quality" of her quilt and feels her scene is "anywhere the viewer wants it to be." When she shuts her eyes on a damp, gray, Pacific Northwest winter day, Jane says, "I conjure up palm tree scenes in my mind. The image stirs up feelings of warmth, dryness, and sunshine, suggesting a touch of the exotic, warming my soul, and lifting my spirits." Jane drew her inspiration from postcards and photos, and a stash of fantastic hand dye-painted fabrics.

Midwinter Tropical Dreamscape by Jane Moxey, Gig Harbor, Washington, 25" × 17", 2002, photograph courtesy of Mark Frey

BASICS

Jane said she was transported and lost all sense of time during the creation of this project. She couldn't wait to get into it each morning. Working intuitively, Jane fearlessly cut and glued her fabrics to her canvas, feeling like the "fabric itself helped me compose a dramatic sky and seascape." Using my methods and inspired by Melody Johnson's free and colorful approach to quickly make small art quilts, Jane said, "I tried my wings and flew." An enlarged black-and-white photograph of palm trees helped her with placement. Jane used a piece of hand-dyed fabric backed with fusible web for the palm trees. Free-motion embroidery suggests filtered sunlight. Jane embroidered hand-dyed perle cotton threads on the water, suggesting movement, and machine quilted her piece.

MATERIALS

- Stabilized muslin canvas: 31" x 23"
- Sky, multicolored reds, scarlets, deep yellows: ½ yard
- Water, multicolored blue/green/purple: ½ yard
- Palm trees and land, multicolored dark brown, olive: ½ yard

- Binding and sun, bright yellow: ⅜ yard
- Backing and sleeve, tropical print: 1 yard
- Batting: 28" x 20"
- Optional: Fusible web: ½ yard
- Variety of rayon, cotton variegated, silk, and hand-dyed threads

CUTTING

Binding: Cut three 2½" strips of bright yellow.

Sleeve: Cut one 8½" strip of tropical print.

CONSTRUCTION

Design, Cut, Glue, and Baste

1. Follow the basic instructions for creating a canvas as described in Chapter One.

2. Prestarch water, sky, and sun fabrics.

3. Cut, position, and pin the sky fabric onto the canvas.

4. Cut, position, and pin the water fabric onto the canvas, using the photograph of the quilt as a placement guide.

5. Cut, position, and glue the sun into place onto the canvas.

6. Cut, position, and glue land "spits" into place onto the canvas.

7. Draw or copy the palm tree shapes, enlarging or reducing as necessary to fit.

8. Trace palm trees onto dark brown fabric. Cut, position, and glue into place.

9. Baste the entire composition with invisible thread.

tip

Starching the fabric heavily or using fusible web makes cutting the serrated palm fronds easier.

MACHINE EMBROIDERY AND PAINTING

1. Add texture to the palm trees with free-motion machine embroidery or use a programmed computer embroidery satin stitch.

2. To give the appearance of sunlight filtering through the palm fronds, highlight with free-motion machine embroidery as shown in the photograph.

3. Embroider large running stitches in the water with variegated hand-dyed pearl cotton threads, to suggest movement.

4. Using orange silk thread, machine quilt across the sun with small, short stitches.

5. Follow the Fine Finishing Techniques as described in Chapter Twelve to complete your quilt.

CHEESEBURGER IN PARADISE

inspiration

A Jimmy Buffet fan, Jan created this vest as a tribute to Jimmy and to his entourage of "parrot head" fans. An award-winning wearable artist, Jan used a commercial vest pattern and, created this work of art in two weeks! Incorporating a variety of motif fabrics, she built her design from the top down on a blue background. Jan said, "I wanted my vest to have a real tropical feel so I used almost all tropical flowers to fill in the bottom portion of the vest, tucking in woodies and surfboards to give the vest an endless summer feel."

Cheeseburger in Paradise by Jan Hayman, El Cajon, California, 2002, photograph courtesy of Jan Hayman

Back view of vest

BASICS

Before assembling the vest, Jan glued the motifs to the blue background fabric using spray adhesive, then machine basted the motifs to the background with invisible thread. She thread-painted or embroidered the elements with "glitzy thread." Jan softens and adds texture to her garments by tossing the sections into the washing machine before stitching the vest sections together.

Hawaiian Escape

Hawaiian Escape by Cindy Walter, Sammamish, Washington, 34" × 29", 2001

inspiration

Created specifically for an appearance on the popular quilting program, *America Sews*, Cindy's quilt recalls memories of leisurely days spent in paradise. Cindy is an accomplished author, teacher, and lecturer who travels across the globe sharing her best-selling *Snippet Sensations* and *More Snippet Sensations* techniques (see Bibliography).

BASICS

Cindy's design process is similar to mine, but she uses fusible web to hold her cut elements into place. Referring to her method as "painting on fabric," Cindy cuts and bonds a myriad of fabrics to create an image, often using her own photographs as inspiration.

UPCOUNTRY GRACE

inspiration

A past program chair for the Maui Quilt Guild, Dianna asked me to teach and lecture during a recent trip to Hawaii. Dianna described the inspiration for her stunning quilt: "Each spring, the Jacaranda trees in upcountry Maui bloom and blanket the country-side with their delicate lavender blossoms and it is one of my favorite times of the year." An intersection where five jacaranda trees are located has been aptly named, "Five Trees," and is one of the most widely reproduced scenes on Maui. As her inspiration, Dianna used a notecard with a watercolor painting of *Five Trees* by Maui artist, David Warren. Dianna's quilt was also featured in a book focusing on contemporary Hawaiian quilt artists.

Upcountry Grace by Dianna Grundhauser, Makawao, Maui, Hawaii, 53" × 37", 2001, photograph courtesy of David Watersun, inspired by a watercolor painting by David Warren. From the collection of John and Leontina Elder

BASICS

Knowing that she wanted to make a landscape quilt of the "Five Trees" one day, Dianna began collecting fabrics long before she took my workshop. Using my motto of bartering, begging, or borrowing from classmates when you don't have the right fabric, Dianna's quilt quickly took shape once she "liberated" the perfect hand-dyed sky fabric from a fellow student. After the landscape was complete, the thought of hand and silk ribbon embroidery nearly sent Dianna over the edge. Instead she loaded some beautiful hand-dyed, six-strand embroidery floss into her bobbin and stitched, using reverse machine embroidery. She quilted her landscape on her longarm quilting machine.

tip

Use a wonderful variety of fabrics in the same color family, but in different values, for the blossoms on the jacaranda trees. The value differences really enhance the blossoms.

inspiration

Wild Thing by Rosellen Carolan, Kent, Washington, 50" × 42", 2001, inspired by Henri Rousseau's 1891 painting, *Tropical Storm With a Tiger*

Intrigued and inspired by Henri Rousseau's painting, *Tropical Storm With a Tiger*, Rosy challenged herself to interpret the feeling it represented in a quilt. As her quilt took shape, she wondered, "What are those strange plants? What is the tiger stalking? Is he being chased or just seeking safety from a storm? What would it be like to have the tiger chasing me?" Facing the dilemma of translating the painting using fabrics in her stash, Rosy created a realistic landscape with a jungle feel and a ferocious tiger. An award-winning, published artist, she says, "I enjoy the freedom of using free-cut, raw-edged appliqué to develop an image, and the ability to move and reposition the pieces until I have it just right."

BASICS

Rosy commented that developing the proper perspective and finding, adapting, and placing fabrics in varied scale to give the correct dimension and depth was vitally important in her quilt. She created her tiger by sandwiching the tiger fabric, polyester organza, and an iron-on tear-away stabilizer. Details were free-motion machine embroidered and the edges zigzag stitched before the tiger was cut out and the stabilizer removed. The tiger was positioned, glued into place, and the remainder of the foliage added.

tip

Create elements as separate units so mistakes can be corrected before the element is a permanent part of the quilt. Iron tear-away stabilizer onto polyester organza and attach the stabilized organza to the back of the fabric with temporary spray adhesive.

WINTER WONDERLAND

Winter Wonderland by Joyce R. Becker, 67" × 43", 2002, photograph courtesy of Mark Frey, inspired by a photograph by Willard Clay

inspiration

Willard Clay's photograph of an old weathered barn, surrounded by towering, snow-covered trees, captivated me from the moment I saw it. With Mr. Clay's permission, my interpretation, *Winter Wonderland*, was created. After locating the ideal sky fabric from Mickey Lawler's SkyDye website (see Resources), and a terrific wood-like fabric for the trees from my stash, my design progressed at record speed.

BASICS

Although this is one of my largest quilts, it was relatively easy to design and build on the canvas. To duplicate the weathered barn, purchase a mottled taupe fabric and then paint it with opaque white textile paint. Once your background fabrics are placed on the canvas, determine the height of the trees and cut them to size with a rotary cutter, using the photograph of the quilt as a reference. Cut a few sample trees until you get the hang of it, then let yourself go! Using a thread that matches the tree-bark, machine embroider skinny twigs and branches, integrating them with the fabric branches and twigs. The fluffy snow is comprised of a layer of white cotton sateen with elliptical shaped overlays of a shadowy commercial fabric, topped with molded batting and white tulle. The wire between the fence posts is thin, silver cording, couched into place with invisible thread.

MATERIALS

- Stabilized muslin canvas: 61" x 37"
- Sky, light gray: 1 yard
- Snow, white cotton sateen: 1 yard
- Shadows in snow, gray, icy blue: ¼ yard
- Overlay for snow, white tulle: 1 yard
- Bark-like dark to medium brown for trees, fence posts: ¾ yard
- Barn and windmill, taupe: ½ yard
- Thin, shiny silver cording for fence post wire: 6 ½ yards
- Batik, taupe for borders and binding: 1¾ yards

- Mottled white, with icy blue spots for backing and sleeve: 3⅛ yards
- Thin white batting for molded snow: 1 yard
- Batting: 70" x 46"
- Textile paint: white opaque
- Artist paint brush: Large
- Shiny, metallic silver and white threads for ice on tree boughs
- Thread for tree-bark
- Variegated thread for vegetation, yellow and brown
- Threads to match fabric for sky and snow

CUTTING

Border: Cut six 6 ½" strips.

Binding: Cut seven 2½" strips.

Sleeve: Cut two 8½" strips.

CONSTRUCTION

1. Follow the basic instructions for creating a canvas as described in Chapter One.

2. Prestarch all fabrics, except sky and cotton sateen.

3. Press sky fabric until all wrinkles and puckers disappear.

4. Use the photograph of the quilt as a guide to position the sky fabric onto canvas.

5. Position the snow fabric onto canvas, using the photograph of the quilt as a guide.

6. Baste around the entire perimeter of the quilt with invisible thread and across the top edge of the snow.

7. Draw, enlarge, then trace the barn onto the taupe fabric.

8. Paint the barn with white opaque textile paint to achieve a weathered look. Dry and heat set.

9. Cut out the barn. Position and glue it into place.

10. Draw, enlarge and trace the windmill onto the taupe fabric.

11. Cut the windmill from the fabric. Position and glue it into place.

tip

Lift the top edge of the barn and slide the base of the windmill under the barn to eliminate any blunt edges.

12. Baste the barn and windmill to the canvas.

13. Using the photograph of the quilt as a reference, eyeball the size of each tree. Cut, position, and glue the trees onto the canvas, starting in the middle and working out to the sides.

14. Using scraps from the tree fabric, cut, position, and glue boughs, limbs, and skinny tree branches. Refer to the quilt photograph for guidance.

tip

Baste the trees, boughs, limbs, and branches immediately, before they move or fall off of the canvas.

15. Cut, position, and glue the fence posts into place.

16. Use the photograph of the quilt as a reference. Position the thin, silver cording for fence wires, and couch with invisible thread.

17. Cut, position, and glue into place the elliptical shapes using the gray and icy blue shadow fabric for the snowy foreground.

18. Place an overlay of batting over the top of the snow fabrics, molding it around the shadows, so the fabric peeks through the batting. Refer to the photograph of the quilt for guidance. Bring the batting up over the bottom of each tree trunk, shredding or tearing it slightly. Mold the batting over portions of the lowest fence wire so the wire is partially covered by the snow.

19. Place an overlay of white tulle over the batting.

20. Baste the snow layers together using invisible thread. Use just enough basting to hold the snow in place. Sew long lines of stitching in a gentle, curving, and random fashion to imply snowdrifts.

21. Trim the excess tulle.

22. Baste the remaining portions of the quilt.

23. Use matching or invisible thread to satin stitch the barn onto the design.

Machine embroider the thin branches.

Machine embroider ice using shiny metallic white and silver threads.

Use white paint to weather the barn.

Stitch the batting and tulle to imply snow drifts.

24. Use matching or invisible thread, an open-toe embroidery foot, and a straight stitch to texture the barn. Follow the direction of the woodgrain to suggest barn siding. Stitch lines that are evenly spaced and close together, so the barn will not shift or sag.

25. Satin stitch the windmill with matching or invisible thread.

MACHINE EMBROIDERY AND PAINTING

1. Machine embroider the skinny tree limbs and twigs to the trees with a matching thread.

2. Use shiny, metallic threads to machine embroider ice onto tree boughs, limbs, and twigs.

3. Machine embroider vegetation around and between the fence posts.

Detail, *Winter Wonderland*

4. Paint snow onto the trees, using the photograph as a guide. Dry and heat set the paint.

5. Follow the Fine Finishing Techniques in Chapter Twelve to complete your quilt.

tip

When machine quilting snow, stitch over the existing basting lines with white thread.

Heading Out by Allison Aller, Washougal, Washington, 36" x 17", 1999, photograph courtesy of Bill Bachhuber

inspiration

Using her skills as a former design student, Allie said her quilt basically "came together by itself." *Heading Out* is the fourth in a series of quilts Allie made while visiting a ranch in northern New Mexico. The quilt was designed and on the wall in an astonishing hour and a half! Allie laughingly said "creating this quilt was exhilarating" because she had the appropriate desert fabrics on hand and felt comfortable with the scale and perspective. Saying the "process of creating small landscapes is more important than the finished product," Allie enjoys making her quilts truly representational. And, although difficult to achieve, she likes to include a light source in her quilts. Allie's striking quilt was featured at the Mariposa Gallery in Santa Fe, New Mexico.

BASICS

As in her quilt, *Port Townsend Autumn* featured in Chapter Six (page 46), Allie prefers sandwiching her backing, batting, and muslin canvas before assembling her collage-style quilt. When the design is complete she stitches through all three layers, usually with invisible thread.

tips

Instead of using spray glue to temporarily hold the fabric pieces on the canvas, use a fabric glue stick.

HIGHLAND FAREWELL

inspiration

Listening to a beautiful trilogy of Scottish music, Sonia said, "I began to imagine the misery of those exiled during the 'Highland clearances,' standing on the ship decks, saying farewell to their beautiful land." To Sonia, this quilt conveys a "certain sadness and yearning, with the rainbow giving hope for a better day." An award-winning, published artist, Sonia's unique interpretations typically have a deeper meaning, often including symbols or hidden messages. The challenge in *Highland Farewell* was to create a credible rainbow. Sonia "enjoyed giving this quilt a Scottish flavor" by incorporating Celtic embroidery and appliquéd thistles.

Highland Farewell by Sonia Grasvik, Seattle, Washington, 47" × 41", 2001, photograph courtesy of Mark Frey

BASICS

Sonia uses techniques similar to mine, but combined the machine embroidery and quilting steps after the quilt was sandwiched. The castle and thistles were made separately and attached after the piece was quilted.

tip

Make some of your appliqué elements separately. Iron a tear-away stabilizer onto a piece of polyester organza, trace your shape on the fabric, and then satin stitch the element to the design. Remove the tear-away stabilizer and carefully melt any remaining fuzzies with a lighter. The thistles and Celtic critter were made using these techniques.

WINTER WOODS: GRANDFATHER TREE

Winter Woods: Grandfather Tree by Cornelia Jutta Forster, Pelham, New Hampshire, 36" x 24", 2001, photograph courtesy of David Caras

Detail, *Winter Woods*

inspiration

"From original inception to the final stitch," this dramatic quilt was completed in one month! Cornelia wanted to "capture in this landscape the sense of that internal strength and energy beneath the serene and stark exterior of winter." Her "lifetime of enjoying trees and winter" and a "love for the meditative aspect of creating landscape quilts," helped Cornelia with dramatic fabric choices and surface design techniques that add depth, texture, and realism.

BASICS

Cornelia's landscape scenes are built on a muslin canvas. She used an enlarged line drawing as a guide. Instead of gluing her elements, Cornelia used a fusible web. She spends a lot of time assessing her quilt during the design process, asking herself, "Is my focal point really focal? Do the minor design elements support, not compete with, the focal point? Is there an interesting movement of value throughout the quilt? Does my eye move across the quilt? And are there any 'dead' areas?" She layered her sandwich, fusing the muslin to the backing and completed the zigzag and free-motion stitching in one step.

tip

Use upholstery and interior design fabrics in your landscape quilts. Designer fabrics offer a wonderful array of colors and patterns not typically available in cottons.

FALL

Fall by Joyce R. Becker, 44" × 40", 2001

Detail, *Fall*

inspiration

Fall is my favorite season of the year. I love the crispness the air, and the incredible and intense colors of the changing leaves that decorate the trees and crunch beneath my feet. Fall, to me, celebrates rebirth, change, and the prospect of discovery and growth. Although I began *Fall* with a compilation of visuals from books, magazines, and catalogs, my true inspiration was the hand-dyed background fabric. I knew this dark background fabric would enhance the bright, vivid fall colors in the rest of the scene. My goal was to create a scene that almost beckons you to smell the air, to take a flying leap into the piles of leaves, or to sit under the tree and contemplate the richness of life.

BASICS

In this case, it was not necessary to use a muslin canvas because the stabilized hand-dyed background fabric served as my canvas. Once the stabilized background fabric was on the design wall, the next element added was the foreground. To create "piles of leaves," I sprayed a light coating of adhesive on top of the foreground fabric, cutting small snippets of hand-dyed multicolored leaf fabrics and pressing them into place. I placed red netting over the top of the leaves and basted the layers together with invisible thread. The branches of the tree on the left side of the quilt were painted with textile paint and enhanced with machine embroidery.

tip

To make a fence look old, distressed, and weathered, turn the edges back occasionally during the basting process. Your fence will look "less perfect" and more realistic.

NEW ZEALAND ADVENTURE

New Zealand Adventure by Joyce R. Becker, 52" × 36", 2001, inspired by a greeting card photograph by Fay Looney

inspiration

New Zealand is one of the most beautiful places on earth. Fulfilling a dream of a lifetime, my husband and I had the opportunity to travel to the North Island when I taught at the 2001 Quilting Symposium in New Plymouth. We were enthralled by the diverse geography; from picturesque, lush, green farmland complete with grazing sheep and cattle, to scenic snow-covered mountains and sunny, subtropical beaches. New Zealanders are fantastic and gracious hosts, welcoming you into their homes, their lives, and their culture. A breathtaking photograph by Fay Looney inspired *New Zealand Adventure*, reminding me of the poignant moments spent in a truly magnificent country.

BASICS

With each new project, I challenge myself to try something different. Sometimes it might be a technique, other times it might be capturing a mood or portraying the feel of the season. With *New Zealand Adventure*, my challenge was to use only fabrics in my stash. To create a muted sky, I placed several layers of polyester organza and tulle over a commercial sky print. To achieve the correct perspective (lighter in the distance, darker in the foreground), I used both the front and back of several commercial fabrics for the rows of mountains. When necessary, I placed overlays of white tulle over the mountain fabrics to tone down values that were too strong. Two commercial prints were used for the foliage, enhanced by extensive machine embroidery to add texture and dimension. I fussy cut wave-like fabric to suggest waves breaking on the shore, and added white textile paint where necessary. I shredded batting on top of the blue water fabric to suggest gentle waves. A layer of fine, ocean-blue tulle holds the batting in place.

MATERIALS

- Stabilized muslin canvas: 47" x 31"
- Muted sky: 1½ yards
- Mountains, four assorted batiks, light, medium, and dark gray: ½ yard of each (audition both sides of fabrics)
- Water, medium blue: 1½ yards (Look for fabrics with more than one value, implying movement.)
- Waves and foam, white and blue: ½ yard (same value blue as in blue water fabric)
- Overlay, ocean-blue fine tulle: 1 yard
- White polyester organza for water or sky overlays (if necessary): 1½ yards

- White, gray, light-blue tulle or netting for overlays (if necessary for sky, water): 1½ yards
- Foliage, two dark greens: ½ yard of each
- Thin white batting for wave overlay: ½ yard
- Dark gray batik for outer border, binding, backing, and sleeve: 3½ yards
- Mottled blue for inner border: ½ yard
- Batting: 55" x 39"
- Textile paint: Pearl-white
- Artist paintbrush: Large
- Threads to match fabric
- Variegated green and yellow embroidery thread

CUTTING

Inner border: Cut five 2" strips from mottled blue fabric.

Outer border: Cut six 5" strips from dark gray batik.

Binding: Cut five 2½" strips from dark gray batik.

Sleeve: Cut two 8½" strips from dark gray batik.

CONSTRUCTION

1. Follow the basic instructions for creating a canvas as described in Chapter One.

2. Cut and pin the pressed sky fabric to canvas.

3. If desired, pin organza and/or tulle overlays over the sky fabric.

4. Pin the water fabric onto canvas. Refer to the photograph of the quilt for placement.

5. Stitch the water and the sky to canvas using invisible thread.

6. Cut and audition each row of mountains. Remember to use the reverse side of fabrics, or use overlays to achieve perspective (lighter in the distance, darker in the foreground).

7. Position and glue each row of mountains into place.

8. Cut small wave-like shapes of foamy, swirling fabric. Position and glue into place. Baste mountains and small waves.

9. With your design on the working wall, and referring to the photograph, add more waves or foam with pearl-white textile paint. Dry and heat set the paint.

10. Shred or tear the batting as an overlay on top of the water to imply waves. Portions of the blue water should show through the shredded batting. Glue into place.

11. Cover the shredded batting with a layer of fine, ocean-blue tulle to hold the batting in place.

Add detail with textile paint, shredded batting, and machine embroidery.

12. Using the photograph of the quilt as a reference, cut dark green foliage shapes. Position and attach the shapes with glue. Details may be added later with machine embroidery.

13. Baste with invisible thread

14. Machine embroider, using matching thread, to highlight each row of mountains, and to add crevices, if desired.

15. Add details to foliage with machine embroidery using a variegated green and yellow embroidery thread. Match the thread to the value in the foliage.

16. Press aggressively from the back with lots of steam.

17. Follow the fine finishing techniques as described in Chapter Twelve to complete your quilt.

Bristlecone by Sandy Bosley, Bothell, WA, 46" × 39", 2000, photograph courtesy of Mark Frey

BRISTLECONE

inspiration

Enchanted by the expansive, open scenery of the ancient Bristlecone Forest, located in the White Mountains of California, Sandy used her own photographs as inspiration for her visual masterpiece. She feels her quilt really captures the essence of the sparse, high altitude location. When creating landscapes, Sandy's desire is to create work that "allows me to visually walk into the scene and find myself there, within the piece."

BASICS

An accomplished landscape artist, Sandy began her design with a simple line drawing, enlarged to full size. When necessary, she used the drawing to make freezer paper templates to get the correct size and scale for her landscape elements. Rather than building her design on a canvas, Sandy sandwiched the backing and batting, and glued her landscape elements directly to the batting, stitching through all three layers.

tip

After trimming the raw edges, clean up your landscape quilt by wrapping two or three layers of masking tape, sticky-side out, around four fingers to create a lint remover. Roll it over the surface, and loose threads and fabric fragments disappear in a flash!

I Will Lift Up Mine Eyes Unto the Hills

inspiration

I was commissioned by the families of Martha Jakle and Martha Koster to create a landscape quilt for display in the narthex of the Silverdale Lutheran Church. My mission was to capture the essence of the Olympic Mountains in Western Washington. My challenge was to realistically mirror the scene as viewed from the entrance of the church. I researched my subject material in great detail at the library.

I Will Lift Up Mine Eyes Unto the Hills by Joyce R. Becker, 66" × 47", 1999, photograph courtesy of Karen Perrine, from the collection of the Silverdale Lutheran Church

Basics

When creating this quilt, I gave myself permission to invent new methods to reach my goals. I experimented with dye painting, stamping, overlays, textile paint, and extensive machine embroidery. I molded dryer lint and covered it with tulle to create crevices on the mountains, adding texture and dimension. This quilt inspired me to take risks and discover new pathways, pushing me to a higher level of creativity.

tip

Use a commercial print for the deer, adding "fur-like" fabric over the print. The boughs were stamped with a commercial stamp using green textile paint. Extensive machine embroidery over the boughs added texture.

Detail of *I Will Lift Up Mine Eyes Unto the Hills*, photograph by Joyce R. Becker

Lake Grasmere by Melissa Anderson, Wellington, New Zealand, 40" × 28", 2002, photograph courtesy of Gilbert van Reenen, inspired by a photograph by Peter Morath

inspiration

A truly inspiring quilt, Melissa's stunning representation is colorful and detailed. It invites you to take a closer look and become a part of the scene. This quilt was featured at a special "Unique New Zealand" exhibit at the 2001 International Quilt Festival in Houston, Texas. Needing little guidance during a workshop I taught in New Plymouth, New Zealand, Melissa said, "I enjoyed the freedom to cut out the fabric pieces and place them quickly on the wall, playing to get them right." She said she has been "really surprised and overwhelmed by the number of men who have quite literally raved over this quilt," attributing it to the realistic appearance versus a geometric pattern of more traditional quilts.

BASICS

Melissa used my methods of design and construction for her quilt. Because she didn't extensively machine quilt her piece, Melissa was able to skip the blocking step in Chapter Twelve after sandwiching and quilting.

tips

Always use a ruler for the horizon line of any water scene; it must be exactly straight.

A toothpick is a fantastic tool to add glue under edges that are "fluffy" or rippled, and to flatten the edges.

Chapter Twelve FINE FINISHING TECHNIQUES

This chapter deals with the Fine Finishing Techniques that ensure your landscape quilt looks good and hangs nicely. You've invested a lot of time designing and creating a stunning landscape design. It is equally important to invest the same energy in the finished appearance of your quilt. Strict attention to the methods regarding Fine Finishing Techniques will pay off. Your quilt will hang straight, with no wobbly edges or ripples. In this chapter you will learn how to square your quilt top, audition and attach borders, make a label on the computer, machine quilt, block, bind, and add a sleeve to hang your quilt.

Squaring Your Quilt Top

Before attaching borders to your quilt top, you **must** square your quilt. If you skip this critical step, your quilt will look lopsided and never hang flat or straight. Your quilt top needs to have precise 90°-angled corners in order to hang correctly. The following are the steps for squaring your quilt.

1. Press the back of your quilt top **aggressively** with steam, as instructed on page 30.

2. Place your quilt top **face down** on a cutting mat. (Olfa makes a three-clip mat that measures 70" x 34".) When you use a large cutting mat, squaring is much simpler.

tip

Placing your quilt top face down helps reduce hysteria as you trim off the edges of your beautiful quilt. My husband frequently says, "But, Joyce, you cut off half of a beautiful tree" (or whatever bites the dust) as I square my quilt. Remember, you made your canvas 3" larger on each side just for this purpose.

3. Using a large ruler, square one corner of your design with a rotary cutter, positioning the markings on your ruler so there is a perfect 90° angle.

4. Turn your quilt top a quarter turn and repeat the same process on the next corner.

5. Use a straight-edge ruler to line up and trim the quilt top between the two squared corners.

Square the first corner.

Square the second corner.

Trim between the two squared corners.

6. Repeat the same process for the remaining two corners, and all four sides.

7. Recheck to make sure each corner is a perfect 90° angle; trim as necessary.

8. To determine if your quilt is really square, you must measure your quilt several times. Using a long, straightedge ruler or tape measure, measure every 3" to 4" from side to side and top to bottom, trimming when necessary. Also measure diagonally from each corner.

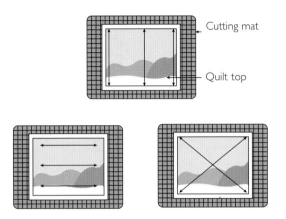

Measure your quilt top and trim as needed to make it square.

To Border, or Not to Border? That Is the Question

There are no hard and fast rules regarding when to include borders on a landscape quilt. Adding borders is a personal choice. A wonderful border treatment can enhance a landscape quilt, framing it as a piece of artwork for the wall. Other times, a border can detract or take away from the mood of the quilt. How do you decide if your quilt needs a border? The solution is simple.

1. Pin your quilt top to your working wall and audition possible border fabrics next to your design. Although you may not have the perfect border fabric in your stash, this step will help you decide if a border is necessary.

2. If you have several fabrics to audition, fold each length of fabric so it is approximately 4" wide. Pin this fabric next to one side of the quilt. Repeat with different fabrics on each of the other sides.

3. Stand back and look at your border choices through a reducing glass.

Auditioning borders

4. Auditioning border fabrics next to your quilt will help you decide whether or not you want to include borders. If you decide you want to add borders, but you don't have an appropriate fabric in your stash, see Fabric Selection for Borders (next page). If you decide not to add borders to your landscape quilt, skip to the Sandwiching and Quilting section that follows. Consider my quilts, *Here Chickee, Chickee, Chickee*; *Patti's Chickens*; and *Chickens Guarding My Secret Garden* (pages 56, 81, 82). Although the quilts are similar in design, I have used different border treatments for the first two quilts, and no border for the third quilt. Borders are subjective. Only you can decide which option works best for your quilt.

Patti's Chickens by Joyce R. Becker, 22" x 24", 2001, from the collection of Patti Cunningham

Fabric Selection for Borders

Selecting border fabric is fun. When shopping for border fabrics, keep the following principals in mind.

1. Use a fabric with various colors and texture, **not** a solid.

2. Select a border fabric that is not too busy or too strong. Your eye should go to the quilt, not the border. Your border treatment should enhance your quilt and not be distracting.

3. Batik fabrics are an excellent choice for borders, as are mottled fabrics, and multicolored fabrics with a lot of movement.

tip

Choose a border fabric that is one value darker than the background or predominant fabric value in your landscape quilt.

4. Select a border treatment after your quilt top is finished. What you think might be a wonderful option at the beginning might not be once the quilt is finished.

5. When shopping for border fabrics, take your quilt top to the quilt shop with you. Hang your quilt top up temporarily in an area with lots of natural light.

Chickens Guarding My Secret Garden by Joyce R. Becker, 24" x 36", 2002, Association of Pacific Northwest Quilters, Pacific Northwest Traveling Exhibit and Auction 2004. Photograph courtesy of Mark Frey

tip

Take a few T-pins with you to the quilt shop so you can temporarily hang your quilt top while auditioning border fabrics.

6. Pull bolts of fabric you think might be appropriate border fabrics. Unroll a yard of fabric from each bolt and position the unrolled fabric next to each side of the quilt top.

7. Step back and take a look. If it's wrong, you'll know it. If it's right, your eye will tell you and the fabric will speak to you, "Buy me, buy me."

tip

Self-bindings or using the same fabric for the binding and outer border fabric enhances landscape quilts. When purchasing the fabric for the outer border, purchase enough for your binding.

Inner Borders

Using a narrow inner border in combination with a wider outer border is a wonderful tool for framing your quilt. A narrow border stops the action of the scene, while a wider border frames the quilt as artwork. Most often, a narrow inner border is an accent color, usually picking up a value or color that is included in your quilt. In *Red Skies at Night, Sailor's Delight* (page 52) the inner border is magenta, accenting one of the colors in the sky.

tip

If the background fabric in your landscape is medium gray, do not select the same value or color for your border unless you add a narrow border using an accent color between the quilt and the outer border. The values will fade together and there will be no definition between the quilt top and the border. Audition narrow border fabrics next to your quilt top, with the wider border fabric positioned on the outside edge.

Auditioning an inner and an outer border

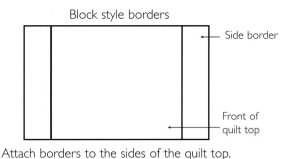

Attach borders to the sides of the quilt top.

Then attach borders to the other two sides of the quilt.

Border Sizes

There is no formula for creating the perfect border width for your landscape quilt. Each quilt is different. On larger quilts, the outside borders should range from 4" to 6". On smaller landscapes, borders are often 4" or less. To determine correct border sizes:

1. Pin your landscape quilt on your working wall.

2. Fold a length of border fabric so it is 4" wide. Hang this piece of fabric next to one side of your quilt.

3. Fold another length of border fabric so it is 6" wide and hang this piece of fabric on the opposite side of your quilt.

4. Stand back and look at the two options with a reducing glass. Your eye should tell you which option works or if your borders need to be wider or narrower.

5. Repeat the same process with the inner border. Place the inner border between your quilt and the outer border. Inner borders usually range from 1" to 3" wide.

Attaching Borders

Depending on your skill level, there are two methods for attaching borders: mitered or block style. Mitered borders are more difficult. If you are apprehensive, begin with block style borders.

Block Style Borders

1. Measure the two longest sides of your quilt. Since you have squared your quilt properly, this measurement should be the same.

2. Cut two border strips the desired width, and use the measurement above for the length.

3. Place the right sides of the quilt and the border together. Sew the borders to the sides of the quilt using a straight stitch, matching thread, and a ¼" seam allowance.

4. Press the seams toward the border. **Use a dry iron without steam.**

5. Measure the width of your quilt, including borders. Cut two strips the desired width, and use the measurement above for the length.

6. Stitch, following the same directions. Press the seams toward the border.

7. Repeat the same process if you want additional borders.

Mitered Borders

Mitered borders add a finished appearance to landscape quilts, enhancing and framing your quilt as a piece of artwork. Although mitered borders take longer than block style borders, it is worth the effort. Follow the directions to add a mitered border:

1. After determining the width of your border, cut two lengths of fabric approximately 10" longer than the width of your quilt, measured across the top and the bottom (this measurement should be the same).

2. Cut two strips for the side borders 10" longer than the measurement along the length of the quilt.

3. If you are including an inner border, repeat Steps 1 and 2.

4. Before attaching the borders to the quilt top, stitch the inner border to the outer border, using a ¼" seam allowance. Precise stitching is necessary if you want perfect mitered corners. Repeat for the remaining three borders.

Inner and outer border stitched together

5. Press the seam toward the outer border using a dry iron.

6. With right sides together, pin one of the borders to one side of the quilt. Mark ¼" away from each corner.

7. Stitch, right sides together, starting and stopping at the ¼" mark.

8. Repeat for the other side and the top and bottom.

tip

Don't panic because your borders extend beyond the corner of the quilt. The extra fabric is necessary for mitering.

Non-Traditional Miters: I prefer not to stitch the two folded and pressed borders together to create a 45° angle. Instead, I use this method:

1. For the first corner, with borders right side out, fold one side to create a 45° angle. Use a ruler to double-check accuracy. Your corner should be square and a perfect 45° angle. Press with a dry iron.

2. Pin the 45° angle into place or use a thin layer of spray adhesive under the fold line to hold temporarily.

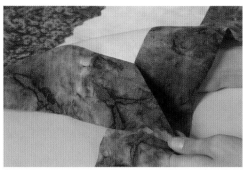

Fold the mitered corner. Check the 45° angle with a ruler.

Creating a 45° angle

3. Stitch along the fold line using a narrow hemstitch with invisible thread and an open-toe embroidery foot. Position the black dot marked on your embroidery foot directly on the fold or pressed line of the fabric.

Stitch the 45° angles closed, using invisible thread and a hemstitch.

4. Repeat for the remaining corners.

5. Trim the excess fabric from each corner. Trim the diagonal seam to ¼".

Trim away any excess fabric from the corners.

Off the Edge

Carrying design elements into the borders of your quilt adds another component of interest in landscape quilts. For example, I carried part of my design into the border of *Red Skies at Night, Sailor's Delight* (page 52).

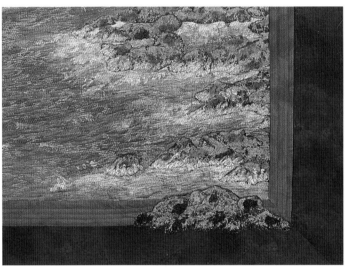
Carrying your design into the border,
Red Skies at Night, Sailor's Delight

1. Stabilize the borders of your quilt prior to beginning this phase of your design, following the instructions in Chapter One. If you skip this step, your border might stretch out of shape or pucker when you stitch.

tip

Stabilizing all of the borders in your quilt helps distribute the weight of the quilt so it hangs evenly.

2. Once you've added the stabilized borders to the quilt top, audition the elements that will "fall off the edge" into the border.

3. Glue the elements into place, once their placement is correct. Stitch with invisible thread, adding machine embroidery, if desired.

Batting Options

In order to lie flat and square, landscape quilts require low-loft battings. I prefer batting that needles well, is soft and pliable, and is the ideal thickness for landscape quilts.

Backing Materials

When selecting a backing fabric, keep these factors in mind:

1. Select a backing fabric that will not show through to the front.

2. Select a backing fabric that enhances your design or the theme of your quilt.

3. Select a backing fabric that will minimize the appearance of the stitches on the quilt back. A fabric that does *not* appear solid from a distance will cover any stitching mistakes. A commercial print is a good choice.

4. Cut your backing fabric 3" larger than your completed landscape quilt top.

5. Press with steam to remove all wrinkles and fold lines.

Sandwiching and Basting Your Quilt

Now that your landscape quilt top is done and the borders are attached, it's time to sandwich the quilt top, batting, and backing together in preparation for machine quilting.

1. Place your pressed backing fabric wrong side up on the floor.

2. Stretch the backing fabric slightly so there are no puckers or wrinkles, but do not pull the backing out of shape. Tape or pin the backing fabric to the floor.

tip

I have commercial-grade carpet in my studio. Using T-pins, I pin the backing fabric directly into the carpet. If you are unable to use T-pins, masking tape is fine.

3. Place the batting on top of the backing fabric, smoothing out any wrinkles or puckers.

4. Place the landscape quilt, right side up, on top of the batting.

5. Stretch and smooth the quilt so there are no puckers or wrinkles, but do not pull the quilt top out of shape. Tape or pin the quilt top to the floor.

6. Baste the quilt with safety pins or thread, beginning in the center of the quilt, and working out. Try to leave no more than 2" to 3" between each basting stitch or safety pin.

tip

Instead of safety pins or thread basting, try the new razor-sharp "forked" basting pins for basting. They work great on any size project!

Basting With Fabric Adhesive

Another option is basting your quilt sandwich together with fabric adhesive. There are several basting glues available. Spray basting is a wonderful option for small projects under 20" x 26". Small projects can be done on a protected worktable, floor, or rug. Follow the same guidelines as for basting with safety pins or thread.

1. Place a vinyl tablecloth on the floor or worktable, vinyl side up. Tape or pin into place.

2. Place the backing fabric, wrong side up, on top of the vinyl tablecloth and tape or pin into place.

3. Spray a thin coat of adhesive directly onto one half of the backing fabric.

4. Fold the batting in half and place half of the batting on the backing fabric with the adhesive. Smooth out any wrinkles or puckers.

5. Spray the other half of the backing fabric and repeat the same process.

6. Spray the top side of the batting and position your landscape quilt onto the batting, smoothing out any wrinkles and puckers.

7. Let the adhesive dry completely before moving the quilt to your sewing machine for quilting.

Labels

Adding a label to your quilt carries on your legacy to future generations. Labels should tell when the quilt was made, who made it, where it was made, the title of the quilt, and if desired, the size.

If your label is stitched on during the machine quilting process, it makes removing it difficult, hopefully discouraging theft of your quilt. I say hopefully, because in spite of these steps, one of my quilts, *La Jolla Tranquility*, is no longer in my possession. I can only hope the new owner cherishes my work.

If you are like me, by the time you are done with your quilt you probably don't want to invest a huge block of time creating a label. Try my slick method for making labels on the computer. Simply scan a portion of your quilt top into a photo program, reduce the size, add text, print it on the computer printer fabric, and your label is done! Chapter Four discusses computer printer fabric in more detail. Samples and instructions follow.

Computer-generated label, *Morning Glories Climbing Over the Gate* by Joyce R. Becker

How to Make Computer-Generated Labels

1. Lift the top of a flatbed scanner.

2. Determine which area is most interesting on your quilt surface and fold your quilt so that area lies face down against the scanner bed.

3. Scan the image into a photo program, such as PhotoShop or Photo Deluxe.

4. Center, crop, and reduce the image to approximately 5" x 7".

5. Add text as described on the previous page, giving the quilt statistics.

tip

Use a font that is easy to read and a text color that enhances your design. Print a sample on plain white paper before printing on the computer printer fabric. Make size, clarity, and color adjustments as necessary.

6. Print the label onto white computer printer fabric.

tip

When you are ready to print, go to the File option on your computer task bar, select Print, then Properties, then Paper Type and select "Other." The printer will make allowances for the additional thickness of the paper.

7. Follow the manufacturer's guidelines for rinsing and heat setting the label.

8. Turn under a seam allowance on each side so the image and text is framed with an equal white border. Press.

9. Baste or pin the label into place along the bottom edge of your quilt, in a corner.

tip

Use invisible thread in the bobbin when machine quilting over the label.

MACHINE QUILTING

If you are like me, you love the look and feel of hand-quilted works of art. I wish that hand quilting was an option for your masterpiece, but it isn't. Sadly, there are just too many layers of fabric and glue to even consider hand-quilting your landscape quilt. Besides, it's amazing how your work of art will be transformed with judicious machine quilting using a variety of threads.

Thread Choices

As with machine embroidery, machine quilting should enhance your design, and your thread choices should reflect the value and color of the element you are stitching. Use any good machine quilting thread, not hand-quilting thread. You can also use rayon or machine embroidery threads, depending on your preference. If you are quilting an area where you don't want the thread to show, such as in the background of my quilt *Fall* (page 74), use invisible thread. In fact, you can machine quilt your entire landscape quilt using invisible thread. Although there are times when you might need to use a lightweight bobbin thread when machine quilting, it is preferable to use the same weight and type of thread that you are using through your needle. The bobbin thread, however, should match your quilt backing.

Stitching Choices

Standard machine quilting techniques that work for more traditional quilts are not suitable for landscape quilts. Just as with the machine embroidery techniques in Chapter Five, machine quilting should enhance your design and therefore, in almost all cases, follow the direction of the element portrayed.

Machine Quilting Options

1. All the quilting on the quilt top should be free-motion stitching.

2. Match the thread to the element you are stitching.

3. Stitch as close as possible to, or over the basting stitches done with invisible thread.

4. Follow the direction and shape of the element.

5. Use the same stitching techniques given in Chapter Five (page 36), duplicating what you see in nature when machine quilting.

6. Trace the elements you are stitching with your needle and thread, adding texture and dimension when desired.

7. Each area of your quilt will require specific quilting. For example, when machine quilting a sky, stipple quilting or quilting in cloud shapes is an option. When quilting water, horizontal stitching, mimicking the flow of water, is desirable. Examples are given in the illustration on page 89 of background stipple (no lines crossing) quilting patterns, horizontal water stitching, cloud shapes, and so on.

8. Quilting around the shape of elements such as flowers or trees without stitching in the middle, will create a "popped out" or almost three-dimensional appearance.

Machine quilting examples for water, mountains, and sky in *New Zealand Adventure* (page 75)

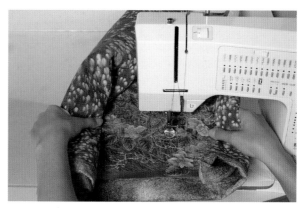

Machine quilting techniques
Hold and manipulate the fabric with your hands while machine quilting.

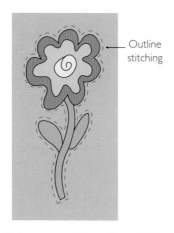

"Pop out" elements with outline stitching.

Outline stitching

Where to Begin

1. Using a machine embroidery needle and a darning foot, prepare your machine for free-motion stitching by lowering the feed dogs. If your machine offers the feature, use the needle-down position.

2. If necessary, roll the edges of your quilt toward the center so your quilt will fit on your work surface area.

tip

Some quilters prefer pinning their quilt edges after rolling while others use bicycle clips to hold the rolled edges down. I simply grasp both rolled edges tightly and manipulate or control the quilting direction with my hands. You may also use a hoop when machine quilting, if desired.

3. Begin stitching in the middle of your quilt and work outward.

4. Pull your bobbin thread to the top, take a few stitches in place and trim the threads.

5. Do a "test run" on a quilt sandwich with a similar thickness of fabric and batting to test tensions and stitching. Adjust, if necessary.

6. You control the rate of stitching, so begin stitching at a medium speed. As you become more comfortable manipulating the fabric, you will be able to stitch faster.

7. After stitching a small area, take a peek at the backside of your quilt. If the stitching is correct, continue. If not, "reverse sew," following the thread-nightmare solutions in Chapter Five (page 38).

8. Quilt equally across the quilt top. If one area is quilted heavily while another is quilted minimally, your quilt will not hang correctly. Your border treatment should also be quilted with equal density.

tip

Remember, thread is fickle. Just because your stitching was wonderful after your initial peek doesn't mean everything is peachy as you continue stitching. Take the time to make sure the stitching on the backside of the quilt remains consistent and acceptable in appearance.

Border Quilting Options

The borders of your quilt set off and enhance your design. Landscape artist Natalie Sewell (page 59), taught me a wonderful trick regarding border quilting.

Since your landscape quilt is artwork, it should be framed like artwork. Instead of just stipple quilting the borders, Natalie frames or "mats" her artwork with narrow straight stitching next to the scene. After the rows of straight stitching, the remaining portion of the border is stipple quilted or stitched free-motion following the motifs on the border fabric.

Framing Stitches

1. Set your machine for straight stitching, feed dogs up, needle-down position, using a walking foot or ¼" foot.

2. Using the width of your presser foot as a guide, stitch the width of one presser foot away from the seam between the border and the quilt scene. Stitch slowly, pivoting when you reach the corners so your lines will be straight and mitered correctly.

3. Sew another frame the width of one presser foot away from the first stitching line. Add additional framing stitches as desired.

4. Quilt the remaining portion of your border using free-motion stipple quilting, or follow the preprinted motifs on the border fabric.

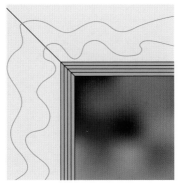

Frame your border with straight stitching and stipple quilting.

Blocking and Quality Assurance

As stated in my introduction, Fine Finishing Techniques in quiltmaking are just as important as the design. When completed, a landscape quilt needs to hang flat and square and be treated as a piece of valuable artwork for display on the wall. A gifted artist, Sonia Grasvik (page 72), shares her remarkable blocking methods to accomplish these tasks.

Blocking

Blocking your quilt "marries" the many layers of fabric together into one cohesive unit. Because there are so many layers of cut and pasted fabrics, coupled with the stabilizer and backing fabrics, blocking your quilt ensures that it will hang flat.

If you skip this step, your quilt may have wobbly or rippling edges!

Supplies and Steps for Blocking

- A large, flannel-backed vinyl tablecloth
- A smooth, white cotton sheet, tablecloth, or a white terry-cloth tablecloth
- T-pins
- Spray bottle filled with water
- Muslin pressing cloth
- Dry iron, **no steam**, set on medium high

1. Place a flannel-backed vinyl tablecloth on a low-loft carpet, flannel side up, smoothing out wrinkles, stretching slightly, securing with T-pins or masking tape.

2. Place a smooth cotton sheet, tablecloth, or terrycloth tablecloth on top of the vinyl tablecloth, smoothing out wrinkles, stretching slightly, securing with T-pins or masking tape.

3. Place your quilt right side down on top of this surface. Smooth out any wrinkles. The quilt should be smooth and flat but **not stretched out of shape.** Secure with T-pins or masking tape on all four corners and several places in between.

4. Spray the pressing cloth with water until it is saturated with water but not dripping wet.

5. Place the wet pressing cloth on one corner of the quilt.

6. Glide your iron across the pressing cloth until the cloth is dry.

7. Rewet the cloth and move it to an adjacent area, iron gently until the cloth is dry. Continue until the entire surface has been blocked.

8. Leave your quilt in this position until all layers are dry. Depending on your climate, this step may take as little as two hours or as much as eight hours.

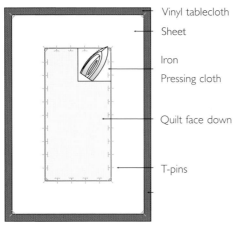

Vinyl tablecloth

Sheet

Iron

Pressing cloth

Quilt face down

T-pins

Block and press your quilt.

1. Hold the binding strips together with a thin coat of spray adhesive.

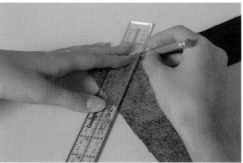

2. Draw a diagonal line from the corner.

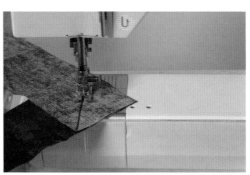

3. Stitch along the line using matching thread; trim the seam to ¼".

Squaring Your Quilt

Follow the squaring instructions given in this chapter. Before attaching your binding, your quilt needs to be squared one last time.

Binding

Once your quilt is square, you are ready to attach your binding. I prefer mitered self-bindings. A self-binding uses the same fabric as the outer border. If your quilt has no border, select a binding that enhances your design and does not blend into the quilt.

Binding Size

Binding size is a personal choice. I prefer a straight-grained, double-fold binding. I do not use bias binding on my landscape quilts.

Binding Steps

1. Use your rotary tools to cut 2½"-wide binding strips. I cannot give you a formula for how many strips to cut because it depends on the quilt size. Start with three strips and cut more if necessary.

2. Join strips together diagonally, as pictured.

tip

When positioning two strips of binding fabric for joining, I use spray glue to hold them in place until stitched.

3. Draw diagonal lines from corner to corner with a pencil and ruler.

4. Stitch along the drawn line with matching thread and trim the seam.

5. Press the seam open with a dry iron.

6. Fold the binding in half with the wrong sides together, and press again with a **dry iron.**

tip

The binding will stretch out of shape if you use steam!

7. Position the binding on the front of the quilt, raw edges together.

To make sure you have enough binding and that the seams do not end up on the corners of the quilt, audition your binding, making adjustments if necessary.

8. Pin the raw edges together at the starting point. Begin stitching 5" away from the starting point, using a ¼" seam, stopping ¼" from the first corner. Backstitch two stitches and trim threads.

Stop sewing ¼" from the corner.

9. Fold the binding up at a 45° angle, as pictured.

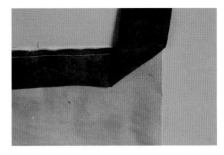

10. Fold the binding down, creating a miter, as pictured.

11. Begin stitching from the edge of the folded corner.

12. Repeat until your binding is attached to the quilt on all four sides. Stop stitching 8" to 10" before reaching your starting point, leaving at least a 3" of overlap.

My friend Debbie White, a gifted miniature quilt artist, taught me the following efficient method for joining together the beginning and the end of the binding strips, with no bulk or unsightly seams.

1. Overlap the ends of the binding. The ending tail of the binding will extend several inches over the beginning tail. Place a straight pin on the ending binding tail, which should be on top, to mark the end of the beginning binding tail. This pin will be used to match up your strips for sewing.

2. Unfold both ends of the binding strips. Place the strips at a right angle to each other with right sides

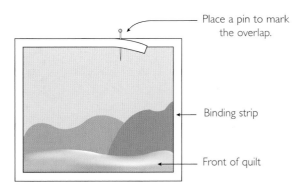

Place a pin to mark the overlap.

Binding strip

Front of quilt

Overlap the ends of the binding strips.

together. The beginning strip (right) should be on top, and extend straight. The ending strip (left) will be behind and should make the turn to form the right angle. Match up the front edge of the beginning strip with the pin on the ending strip. The end of the beginning strip should line up evenly with the side of the ending strip.

3. Glue or pin the two edges into place. With a pencil and ruler, draw a diagonal stitching line from the upper left to the lower right of the overlapped strips. Stitch with matching thread.

4. Trim the seam allowance of the diagonal seam to ¼" and press.

5. Sew the final section of the joined binding to your quilt top. Your binding should fit perfectly with no bumps or lumps!

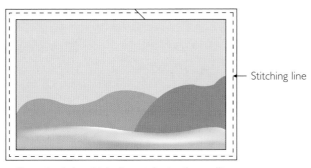

Stitching line

Sew the joined binding strip to the quilt. The binding should be smooth and flat.

6. Turn the binding to the back and blindstitch with thread to match the back of the quilt. Be sure to sew through the backing and batting layers only, so the stitches won't show on the front.

7. Miter the corners as you reach them.

8. Stitch the folded miters closed with matching thread, back and front.

Final Blocking

Sonia Grasvik recommends blocking your entire quilt again after the binding is attached. In a pinch, however, it is perfectly acceptable to just press the binding with a wet pressing cloth.

Attach a Hanging Sleeve

To display your quilt properly on the wall, you need a hanging sleeve.

1. Cut an 8½"-wide strip of fabric to match the back of your quilt.

2. To determine how long to make this strip, measure the width of your quilt and add 3".

3. Wrong side up, fold the short outside edges of the fabric toward the center of the fabric, 1½" on each side. Press with steam. Stitch with matching or invisible thread next to the raw edge.

tip

Hem the edges of the sleeve before making a hanging "tube" so the hanging rod or stick does not get stuck when threaded through the sleeve.

Fold the raw edges 1½" toward the center. Press with steam. Stitch next to raw edge with matching or invisible thread.

4. Fold the strip in half, wrong sides together, with the lengthwise edges meeting. Stitch a ¼" seam with matching or invisible thread.

5. Turn the sleeve or tube right side out and press.

6. Position the sleeve so it is centered and ¼" from the top of the quilt.

7. Whipstitch or blindstitch the bottom edge of the sleeve to the quilt using matching or invisible threads.

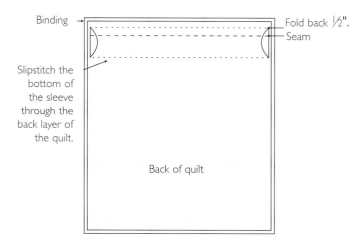

Sleeve is centered and positioned below the binding on the back of the quilt.

8. Instead of stitching the top edge of the sleeve, fold the sleeve back ½" from the top and whipstitch along this line.

tip

When you stitch ½" down from the top edge of the quilt, below the binding, your quilt will hang flat against the wall and the upper binding will not pucker.

9. Purchase a flat stick at the home improvement store. Cut the stick ½" longer than the width of your hanging sleeve. Place eye hooks on the upper edge of the stick next to both ends.

Hanging stick with eyehooks

10. Place the hanging stick in the sleeve and hang, using fine finishing nails.

Quality Assurance

What are quality assurance techniques and why bother? I suspect some of you have attended quilt shows and witnessed untidy quilts—untrimmed threads, edges that were unraveling, a quilt in need of good once over with a sticky lint roller. Use these methods to ensure your quilt is tidy and clean.

1. Place your quilt face-up on a large protected table.

Do not place your quilt directly on a wooden table. Any oil or polish will be absorbed into your quilt! Place a clean, white sheet on your table first.

2. Place a bright light next to your quilt to help with the "examination" process. A floor-model full-spectrum light works great.

3. Because your quilt was done using raw-edge appliqué, there are bound to be some edges that have not been stitched down completely and need to be trimmed. Landscape artist Natalie Sewell calls this giving your quilt a "haircut." Use a sharp pair of embroidery scissors for this process and trim away any frayed edges.

4. Examine your quilt front for stray threads, trimming as necessary.

5. Use a new sticky lint roller to remove all lint, dust, and thread tails from the surface of your quilt.

6. Repeat the same process on the back of your quilt.

Congratulations! You've completed a stunning landscape quilt.

Author's Postscript

What a joy it has been to write this book and share my methodology for creating landscape quilts with you. Sharing my ideas and quilts allows me to give back to a community that continues to bless and enrich my life. I hope that this book inspires you to reach new levels, to take unchartered risks, to play, and above all, to enjoy yourself during the journey! My fondest wish is that you truly do discover a newfound capacity for creativity when making Luscious Landscapes. I love seeing the landscape creations inspired by this book, so please, send me snapshots! Contact information is included with my biography on (page 95). May your creativity continue to soar.

Joyce R. Becker

BIBLIOGRAPHY

Becker, Joyce R., *Nature's Patterns*, Lincolnwood, IL: The Quilt Digest Press, a division of McGraw-Hill, 1996.

Johnson, Vicki L., *Paint and Patches*, Paducah, KY, American Quilter's Society, 1995.

Lawler, Mickey, *Skydyes*, Lafayette, CA, C&T Publishing, Inc., 1999.

Walter, Cindy, *More Snippet Sensations*, Iola, WI: Krause Publications, 2000.

Zieman, Nancy and Natalie Sewell, *Landscape Quilts*, Birmingham, AL: Oxmoor House, Inc, 2001.

At the Cutting Edge: Contemporary Hawaiian Quilting, 2nd ed., Island Heritage, 2003.

RESOURCES

Fabric, dye, and paint supplies
Dharma Trading Co.
P.O. Box 150916
San Rafael, CA 94915
www.dharmatrading.com

Recommended source for Versatex, Setacolor,
and Jacquard Textile Paints
Pro Chemical and Dye
P.O. Box 14
Somerset, MA 02726
www.prochemical.com

Fabric, thread, and quilting supplies
Recommended source for 54" carded cotton
sateen, bleached, Style 428.

Testfabrics, Inc.
P.O Box 26
West Pittston, PA 18643
www.testfabric.com

Hand-dyed fabric by Judy Robertson
Just Imagination
P.O. Box 583
Burlington, WA 98233
Judysfabric@earthlink.net

Thread and KK2000 Temporary Spray Adhesive
Sulky of America
3113 Broadpoint Drive
Harbor Heights, Fl 33983
www.sulky.com

Pellon Fusible non-woven interfacing—sheer
to lightweight fabric
Freudenberg Nonwovens, Pellon Division
3440 Industrial Drive
Durham, NC 27704

Web of Thread
19424 63rd Ave. NE
Kenmore, WA 98028
www.webofthread.com

June Tailor Colorfast Printer Fabric Sheets (white)
Available in most quilt shops

www.junetailor.com

Setaskrib+ Markers
Available through Pro Chemical and Dye
and quilting shops

SKYDYES, Mickey Lawler
P.O Box 370116
West Hartford, CT 06137-0116
www.skydyes.com

505 Spray and Fix (temporary repositional
fabric adhesive)
J.T. Trading Corporation
1200 Main Street
P.O. Box 9439
Bridgeport, CT 06601-9439
Email: order505@aol.com

Material Resources Fabric Collection
Newport Quilt
644 Coast Hwy, Suite B
Newport, OR 97365
www.newportquilt.com

Artfabrik: Hand-dyed
fabrics and thread
Laura Wasilowski
324 Vincent Place
Elgin, IL 60123
www.artfabrik.com

Hoffman Fabrics
25792 Obrero Drive
Mission Viejo, CA 92691
www.hoffmanfabrics.com

Fiskar Softouch Scissors
Model 9911-7097
Available at most quilt shops
www.fiskars.com

Drawing on her life-long love of nature, this award-winning quilt artist says she studies nature as though she is looking through the lens of a camera, setting up possible landscape scenes in her mind for future reference. Her inspirations come from many sources including photographs, greeting cards, and photography books. Joyce incorporates many original, unique, and sometimes unorthodox surface design techniques to impart realism in her landscape quilts.

Photo courtesy of Mark Frey

The author of *Nature's Patterns: Inspirations and Techniques for Quilt Makers*, Joyce became enamored with the landscape genre in 1995 after making a series of landscape watercolor quilts. Because she wanted her landscape quilts to impart realism, Joyce quickly realized she would have to "invent" a method to create landscape quilts in a non-traditional format. Through trial and error, her origina methodology eventually evolved into a fun and easy process. Feeling blessed to have such a creative profession, Joyce focuses her art, writing, teaching, and lecturing on landscape quilts and volunteers throughout the quilting community. She was a founding board member and now an active volunteer of the Association of Pacific Northwest Quilters, sponsors of the bi-annual regional Pacific Northwest QuiltFest exhibit in Seattle, Washington. Joyce is also an active member of the Contemporary Quilt Art Association of Seattle, Washington; the Evergreen Piecemakers Quilt Guild of Kent, Washington; the International Quilt Association; and the American Quilter's Society.

Joyce's quilts have been displayed internationally in contests and invitational exhibits, appearing in books, magazines, and on television. Many articles authored by Joyce have appeared in mainstream quilting magazines, and she has also been featured on HGTV's *Simply Quilts*. The Auburn Arts Commission sponsored her first solo exhibit, held in Auburn, Washington, in 2001.

A California native, Joyce has resided in Kent, Washington, since 1985, where she enjoys spending time with her husband, Donald. In addition to their two sons and a daughter-in-law, Joyce has five grown stepchildren (who affectionately call her "step-monster") and five grandchildren. In her spare time, Joyce enjoys hanging out with her "Thursday Group" quilting buddies, and traveling with her husband.

Joyce's lively sense of humor and positive attitude result in lectures and workshops that inspire, inform, and entertain quilters as she travels throughout the world. If you are interested in a booking, Joyce's website, www.joycerbecker.com, includes up-to-date information. You may e-mail Joyce at Jbecker3@hotmail.com.

INDEX

Artist pencils, 8, 33
Auditioning elements, 24
Background fabric, 13, 19, 82
Backing fabric, 85
Bamboo skewers, 8, 38
Basting, 19, 26, 85–86
Batting, 8, 85
Binding, 90–92
Bleaching, 34
Blocking your quilt, 89–90, 92
Blue Mountains (Joyce Becker), 44–45
Bobbin case, extra, 7–8, 26–27
Bobbin embroidery, 39
Bonding elements onto canvas, 23
Borders, 81–85
Bristlecone (Sandy Bosley), 77
Brushes, for painting, 31, 32
Camera, 9
Canvas, muslin, 9–10, 18–19
Chair, 9
Changing/covering up unwanted
    elements, 24–25
Cheeseburger in Paradise (Jan Hayman), 64
Chickens Guarding My Secret Garden
(Joyce Becker), 56, 82
Clip-art images, printing on fabric, 34–35
COMPUTER
    using for labels, 86–87
    using to create elements for quilt, 34–35
Copyrighted image, 12
Cotton sateen, 31, 35
Couching, holding thread/yarn in place, 51
Cutting shapes, 20–22
Darning foot, 6
DESIGN
    balancing, 25
    choosing, 12
    placement guidelines, 18–19
    simplifying, 11
Designer fabrics, 73
Design wall, 10
Double needle, 55
Dryer lint, adding dimension with, 30, 78
Embroidery, see Machine embroidery
English Garden (Joyce Becker), 38, 41–42
Errors, fixing, 25
Fabric adhesive, basting with, 86
Fabric markers, 8, 33, 34
Fabric, organizing, 9
Fabric printer sheets, 35
Fabrics, selecting, 12–17, 82
Fall (Joyce Becker), 9, 39, 74
Feed dogs, 6
Fences, adding realism to, 74
Finger cots, 36
First Frost (Joyce Becker), 49
Flowers, 9, 15, 23, 48
Foliage, 15, 21

Foreground elements, attaching, 20
Framing stitches, 89
Free-motion foot, 6
Free-motion stitching, 36, 87–89
Fusible web, 9, 23
Fusing, *see* Bonding
Fussy cutting, 22
Gardens, 15, 56–61
Gluing elements onto canvas, 24, 51, 79
Grasses, 9, 33, 38, 48
Hanging sleeve, 92
Hawaiian Escape (Cindy Walter), 65
Heading Out (Allison Aller), 71
Heat setting paint/pencils, 31–32, 34
Here Chickee, Chickee, Chickee (Joyce
    Becker), 56–58
Highland Farewell (Sonia Grasvik), 72
Hoops, using for embroidery, 36–37
Horizon line, using a rule for, 71
Interfacing, fusible, 7, 10
I Will Lift Up Mine Eyes Unto the Hills
    (Joyce Becker), 17, 24, 78
Jerusalem (Natalie Sewell), 59
Kaikoura Rocks (Marie Blennerhassett), 55
Labels, 86–87
Lake Grasmere (Melissa Anderson), 79
Large structures, attaching, 23, 29
Light, full-spectrum, 9
Lint removal, 77, 93
Machine embroidery, 36–39
Machine quilting, 87–89
Midwinter Tropical Dreamscape (Jane
    Moxey), 62–63
Mitered borders, 84
Morning Glories Climbing Over the Gate
    (Joyce Becker), 15, 33, 34, 60
Mountains, 21, 75–79
Needles, sewing machine, 8
Negative space, 12
Netting, see Overlays
New Zealand Adventure (Joyce Becker),
    12, 13–14, 17, 75–77
Organza, see Overlays
Outline stitching, 88
Overlays, using tulle, netting, organza, 17,
    19–20, 30
Paint and Patches (Vicki Johnson), 32
Painting, steps for, 32
Path, creating, 61
Patti's Chickens (Joyce Becker), 56, 81
Pens, fabric, 8, 33, 34
Perspective, importance of, 17, 19–20
Photographing quilts, 25
Port Townsend Autumn (Allison Aller), 46
Preprinted fabrics, 14, 22, 40
Pressing the quilt top, 30
Printer fabric, 35
Projects, size of first, 18, 40

Quilting, *see* Machine quilting
Raw edge appliqué, 26–29
Realism, tools to add, 30
Red Skies at Night, Sailor's Delight
    (Joyce Becker), 31, 52–54, 85
Reducing glass, 8
Road map, for bobbin embroidery, 39
Rocks, 9, 23
Sanctuary (Joyce Becker), 34, 61
Sandwiching quilt layers, 85–86
Scale, of fabric, 14
Scissors, 7
Seascapes, 52–55
Sewell, Natalie, 88–89
Skydyes (Mickey Lawler), 32, 93
Snow, quilting, 70
Spray glue, 7, 24
Sponging, 32–33
SQUARING
    finished quilt, 90
    quilt top, 80–81
STABILIZER, 9, 10
    for borders, 85
Stamping, 33
Starch, 7, 18
Stitching sequence, 28–29
Sunset (Joyce Becker), 43–44
Synthrapol, 34
Table extension, for sewing machine, 7
Tension, adjusting, 27–28, 37
Textile paints, 30–32
Texture, adding, 17
Thread nightmares, fixing, 38
Threads, 8, 26, 36–37, 87
Three-dimensional elements, creating,
    24, 58
Trees, 9, 15, 23
Tropical quilts, 62–67
Tulle, see Overlays
Twilight at Paradise (Joyce Becker),
    47–48
Upcountry Grace (Dianna Grundhauser), 66
Upholstery fabrics, 73
Value, importance of, 13, 24
Vest, Jimmy Buffet (Jan Hayman), 64
Visual interest, creating, 15
Walking foot, 6
Water, 20, 54, 55
Wild and Free (Carol Smith Mackenzie), 55
Wilderness quilts, 68–74
Wild Thing (Rosellen Carolan), 67
Winter Visitor (Rosellen Carolan), 51
Winter Woods: Grandfather Tree
    (Corneilia Jutta Forster), 73
Winter Wonderland (Joyce Becker), 20,
    68–70